Banished & Embraced

To Barbara —
Good wishes from

Jane Forbes

9-15-2018

Mythos Press

"Blessings" Chew Kee Store. *Courtesy Daniel D'Agostini*

BANISHED

&

EMBRACED

The Chinese in Fiddletown

and the Mother Lode

by Elaine Zorbas

MYTHOS
PRESS

2015

Banished & Embraced

The Chinese in Fiddletown and the Mother Lode

Copyright © 2015 by Elaine Zorbas

First edition
First printing

ISBN-13: 978-0-9658793-9-2

Published by Mythos Press
Post Office Box 566
Plymouth, California 95669

Cover: Photo of friends Bob Lawrence and Jimmie Chow, circa 1920. *Amador County Archives*

Printed in the United States of America

CONTENTS

PREFACE
BROKEN RECORD: RESEARCH OBSTACLES 2
JIMMIE CHOW: THE LAST CHINESE OF FIDDLETOWN 5

A DISTANT HOME IN THE SIERRA NEVADA FOOTHILLS
THE GOLD RUSH IN AMADOR COUNTY 8
CHINA ORIGINS AND DEPARTURE FOR CALIFORNIA 11
MINING AND BARRIERS TO THE SEARCH FOR GOLD 15
THE GRISWOLD MURDER, CRIME AND JUSTICE 22
THE RISE OF AMADOR COUNTY CHINATOWNS 32
THE FIDDLETOWN CHINESE COMMUNITY DEVELOPS 35
FIDDLETOWN'S CHINESE HERB DOCTOR: YEE FUNG CHEUNG 41
PROPERTY OWNERSHIP AND TOWN PLANS 51
ENTREPRENEURS AND MERCHANTS 54
FOO KEE, FIDDLETOWN MERCHANT AND LEADER 58
LABORERS AND THE ANTI-CHINESE MOVEMENT 63
CHINESE EXCLUSION AND BOYCOTTS IN AMADOR COUNTY 71

THE FIDDLETOWN EXCEPTION
FIDDLETOWN'S CHINESE POPULATION: THE 1870S 77
FIDDLETOWN CHINATOWN UNDER PRESSURE 79

DAILY LIFE ON GOLD MOUNTAIN
A WEB OF CONNECTIONS: CHINESE ASSOCIATIONS 84
CHINESE WOMEN, MEN AND LIVING ARRANGEMENTS 90
DIVERSIONS: OPIUM & GAMBLING 97
CHINESE CELEBRATIONS AND CUSTOMS TRANSPLANTED 102
FIDDLETOWN'S CHINESE CEMETERY: PORTRAIT OF A COMMUNITY 112

THE CHEW KEE STORE
CHEW KEE, MERCHANT AND GAMBLER 117
FROM FONG CHOW YOW TO JIMMIE CHOW 126

END OF A CENTURY
EXODUS OF THE CHINESE FROM AMADOR COUNTY 139
LAST DAYS OF FIDDLETOWN'S CHINESE COMMUNITY 148
LAST FUNDRAISING FOR THE FIDDLETOWN CEMETERY 153
BURIAL IN FIDDLETOWN, RETURN TO CHINA 155

RENEWAL AND CONTINUITY
JIMMIE CHOW, CHINESE AMERICAN 163
THE YEP FAMILY OF JACKSON 173
THE YEE FAMILY LEGACY 176
PRESERVING THE CHINESE HERITAGE IN FIDDLETOWN 179

POSTSCRIPT

BEGINNINGS: My Path to Fiddletown Chinatown   192

ACKNOWLEDGEMENTS   197

RESOURCES

Maps   201

BIBLIOGRAPHY   208

INDEX

LIST OF MAPS

Map 1.   California counties   202
Map 2.   Guangdong Province, Pearl River Delta   203
Map 3.   Mother Lode - Amador County   204
Map 4.   1870 Fiddletown Townsite Map (East part of town)   205
Map 5.   1870 Jackson Townsite Map (North Main Street)   206
Map 6.   1871 Drytown Townsite Map   207

Dedicated

To the Fiddletown Preservation Society for keeping the Chew Kee Store open and for striving to preserve Fiddletown's historic buildings.

PREFACE

BROKEN RECORD: RESEARCH OBSTACLES

Gathering primary historical information on the Chinese in Amador County or elsewhere presents many problems, especially with language. Chinese immigrants spoke Cantonese, a language with nine tones (changes in pitch) and sounds unfamiliar to the Western ear. Most Chinese immigrants were illiterate, and even those who could read and write signed their names using Chinese characters, indecipherable to Americans. Few Chinese could speak English, and any broken English was often misunderstood and mocked. This left government officials and census takers to interpret the sounds.

Anyone examining Chinese records will find name after name beginning with "Ah"—Ah Choy, Ah Sam, Ah Ping, etc. Officials construed this sound as a last name, when in actuality it was a familiar form of address used by Cantonese speakers to greet each other. The name following the "Ah" was either a first or last name or nickname as used by Chinese speakers. For example, the 1870 Census of Population covering the Jackson area (Township 1) listed eleven people referred to as "Ah Sam," actual surname unknown.

Western custom is to put the surname last. In China, a full name begins with the surname, followed by the first name, leading to great confusion in U.S. public records. Listed the Chinese way, a last name becomes officially a first name, and the first name becomes the last name. For example with the name Sun Yatsen, "Sun" is the surname and Yatsen is the first name. A Chinese middle or second personal name, which sometimes denotes generation, often appears after the first name. An example is the name Fong Chow Yow, where "Yow" is interpreted as the last name in U.S. public records.

In addition in the nineteenth century there were no standards for transliterating Cantonese into English. Americans wrote down what they heard, often incorrectly. Many names were garbled because of sounds unfamiliar to English speakers. The same Chinese name could be spelled different ways in English: Fong or Feng or Fung, Chu or Chew or Chow, Yee or Yi, Kee or Ki, for example. Also many Chinese people were referred to by more than one name depending on their age and station in life. Merchants incorporated the name "Kee," meaning *store*, which was preceded by their first name with no indication of the surname.

Consulting the U.S. Census of Population has often been frustrating, both in using *Ancestry.com* and looking at the actual Census manuscripts, where handwriting could be unreadable. With *Ancestry*, I was able to obtain aggregate population numbers for the different townships and to identify Chinese women residents. But it failed me when I searched by name or occupation, for which there is no search field. In trying to find consistency among the various censuses for Fiddletown's Chinese population, especially its merchants, I was completely baffled by the 1880 Census in which there was not one match with names in previous censuses. A lot depended on the individual census recorder and what he or she heard.

Amador County records for the nineteenth century presented other problems because many sources are missing or not complete. County assessment rolls, so important in identifying property owners and their holdings, exist in full only for 1855, 1856, 1878-79, and 1892 with only indexes for selected years. Business license records from 1863 to 1868 covered only Drytown and small communities at the far north end of the county. Although from 1870 to1885 they encompassed the entire county, records were organized by township only, not by name of the town.

The townships include larger areas than towns, but the coverage varies with each census. For example, the 1860 and 1870 censuses for Township 6 included Fiddletown and the neighboring Shenandoah Valley. After 1882 Fiddletown now identified as a village, became part of Township 3, grouped with other smaller communities.

It was a great challenge for me to attempt to correlate names from various records—deeds, census, business licenses, and tax and property assessment records. With no personal information on Chinese residents in other towns, I tried to piece information together based on disparate records, but the human element is usually missing.

Newspapers become primary sources with time because they reflect the outlook of a particular era. Here, too, there are gaps in Amador County papers. Entire years of local newspaper issues are missing or very spotty, especially in the 1860s. Several years on microfilm at the Amador County Library were missing for the 1880s; fortunately they exist in fragile paper format in the Amador County Archives. I primarily consulted the *Amador Ledger* as the more balanced and descriptive of the local newspapers. Its rival, the *Amador Dispatch*, was pro-South and viciously anti-Chinese.

In the nineteenth century as now, newspapers tended to write about death and destruction. They often sensationalized reports of Chinese vice (opium use, prostitution) which helped build momentum against the Chinese presence in the U.S. Stories and editorials were written in a sneering and contemptuous tone, attacking Chinese race, culture and religion. Chinese were referred to as heathens, Celestials, moon-eyed, Mongolians, John Chinaman, China Mary. From today's perspective these attacks are painful to read. However, I had to keep in mind that the times were different then—ignorance, fear and a pervasive sense of white superiority dominated the national outlook. Amador County is a microcosm of what transpired, taking its lead from other areas that were much more violent and virulent.

It is my intent to give voice and names to the many Chinese people who passed through, worked furiously, contributed to the development of the region, and were forgotten. Few personal stories remain; there are no diaries or journals. This makes the business correspondence, letters, ledgers, books, and artifacts from Fiddletown's Chew Kee Store a rich source of documentation of a closely linked Chinese community.

Note: The Chinese language does not have an alphabet with letters that are associated with sounds used to form words. Written Chinese uses characters in which each symbol represents a separate word or meaning. There are over 5,000 characters in Chinese, each of which requires memorization. Cantonese and Mandarin are distinct spoken languages, both using the same written characters. Since Chinese immigrants spoke Cantonese, the spelling in this book of Chinese names of individuals and places is based on that pronunciation as commonly spelled using Roman letters; Mandarin pronunciation using Pinyin Romanization appears in parentheses. The exception is current use of Pinyin spelling for Guangdong (Canton Province), Guangzhou (Canton City) and Qing (Ching) Dynasty. The U.S. Census of Population is referred to as the Census. Words in [ ] brackets are added by the author.

JIMMIE CHOW: THE LAST CHINESE OF FIDDLETOWN

Figure 1. Jimmie Chow portrait. *Amador County Archives*

This history begins and ends with the story of Jimmie Chow. He is a legend in Fiddletown. For more than forty years, he was the sole representative of the close Chinese community that had once populated this small gold mining town in the Sierra Nevada foothills of California. A quiet and kind man, skilled in many trades, he was loved and mourned by the residents of the community who cared for him in his later years. When he died in 1965 at the age of eighty he was the only person of Chinese ancestry to be buried in the Fiddletown public cemetery.

He was born as Fong Chow Yow (Feng Qiu You) in 1885, during the height of discrimination against Chinese immigrants. Then, almost every town in Amador County and most of California had a definable Chinese section. By the beginning of the twentieth century, few Chinese people were left in the gold country; most had departed for China or large cities such as San Francisco or Sacramento.

Jimmie stayed in Fiddletown and adapted to American culture, yet he never lost his Chinese heritage. He bridged both cultures. He left a legacy in Fiddletown's Chew Kee Store, where he lived for most of his life. Thanks to his frugality, the store is furnished with hundreds of objects of Chinese daily life, reflecting the various residents of the store: the herb doctor Yee Fung Cheung, the merchant Chew Kee and his wife Sigh Choy, and Chow himself. Now a museum, the Chew Kee Store evokes the lost past of early Chinese immigrants who contributed so much to California.

Jimmie Chow was emblematic of the thousands of Chinese people who tried to make a life in California during and following the Gold Rush. There were many obstacles and few opportunities, decades of unremitting labor, yet strong social and cultural ties created a network of connections among Chinese people estranged from the larger society. If there is one quality that distinguishes the Chinese who ventured to California, it is resilience.

Fiddletown does not stand alone. The surrounding towns of Amador County reflected the broader context, the creation of Chinatowns that were ubiquitous throughout California as well as the anti-Chinese movement that aimed at expelling Chinese immigrants from the U.S. This work focuses on Fiddletown and the residents of the Chew Kee Store, while examining Chinese life and culture in that broader context. Fiddletown remains unique in many ways, not just because so much remains from its Chinese past but it also stands out as a place of companionship and safety for Chinese residents during hard times.

A Distant Home in the Sierra Nevada Foothills

THE GOLD RUSH IN AMADOR COUNTY

The land in northeast California that became Amador County is situated between two rivers, the Cosumnes and the Mokelumne, its rolling foothills rising east towards the mighty Sierra Nevada mountain range. Prior to the discovery of gold in early 1848, the terrain was sparsely settled by the Miwuk tribe of Native Americans who lived in communities near creeks, sustaining themselves with game hunted from the forests around them, fish from the rivers, and acorns gathered from abundant oaks. Hills were thickly wooded with oaks, cedars, and lofty pines; streams, creeks, and rivers ran clear, some filled with salmon and trout.

The Mokelumne River, which originates high in the Sierra Nevada, drew miners to excavate its banks, bars and riverbed starting in the early years of the Gold Rush. It became the dividing line between two counties, when Amador County split off from Calaveras County in 1854. The town of Jackson had already claimed the title of county seat prior to the separation. A year later, Fiddletown joined Amador County, annexed from El Dorado County to the north with the Cosumnes River as the northern divider.

The Gold Rush started an upheaval, literally and figuratively. Beginning 1848, thousands of would-be miners made their way to California's foothills, heaving up earth, digging deep holes in mountains and ravines, damming up and diverting rivers—all in the search for flecks and nuggets of gold, known as placer deposits, extracted from dirt and gravel deposited over millions of years in both flowing and dry ancient rivers. Camps consisting of tents were hastily assembled and then abandoned as miners moved to the next promising spot. Gambling was ever present in the mining camps, which were mostly occupied by men. The first miners in this area were Californios, Mexicans, Americans, Chileans, and Native Americans, who were later joined by others from countries around the world. By the time that Chinese arrived in numbers, much of the placer gold had already been extracted.

Some mining camps evolved into towns, populations swelling in the early to mid-1850s. As scarce supplies were brought into the wilderness, merchants charged high prices and fared better than most miners. The towns acquired a number of shops to service the growing communities— general merchandise stores, groceries, blacksmith shops, livery stables, hotels, restaurants, boarding houses, dance halls, saloons, gambling joints,

Figure 2. Lithograph of Jackson in 1857. *Amador County Archives*

brothels, barber shops, butcher shops, express offices and in some cases, breweries. As more families settled in the area, schools and churches were established as well as post offices and fraternal organizations. Structures for the most part were built of wood, the most abundant and highly combustible material. Towns were periodically destroyed by fire and flood and then rebuilt. More expensive buildings that survived were constructed of brick or stone with iron doors and windows to protect the interior from fire.

Drytown, on a trail leading from Sacramento into the Sierra foothills, was one of the earliest settlements. From north to south Amador City, Sutter Creek and Jackson lined up, each town located next to creeks and close to rich veins of gold-bearing quartz known as the Mother Lode, where millions of dollars of gold were extracted from deep shaft mines. The Ione Valley, situated about twelve miles west of Jackson, was a verdant area with fertile soil and tall grasses ideal for cattle ranching and agriculture. Ione City was established in 1853. In the southwest part of the county, Lancha Plana developed next to the Mokelumne River.

To the east at higher altitudes, the town of Volcano, located in a flat grassy plain surrounded by mountains (mistaken for a volcanic caldera), boomed with placer mining in the early Gold Rush. Starting in 1852, the road conducting emigrants from the East over the Sierra Nevada branched into a fork that led pioneers to Volcano, greatly increasing its population and mining activity. Fiddletown was located in the hills in the northeast part of the county on a road that led from Sacramento, with stage stops at Volcano, attracting miners to its rich placer deposits. In the 1870s, Plymouth, six miles west of Fiddletown rose to prominence with the establishment of several industrial gold mines, also along the Mother Lode belt of quartz veins. All of these towns have survived into the twenty-first century, with the exception of Lancha Plana which was in ruins long before it was inundated by the Camanche Reservoir in 1963. Other towns and encampments in the county that once thrived have disappeared.

CHINA ORIGINS AND DEPARTURE FOR CALIFORNIA

"Gold for the taking!" By 1849, this cry reverberated around the world and changed the destiny of California. It spread through the United States, Chile, Mexico, the countries of Europe, Australia and China. Men with dreams of easy riches and a better life left their families at home and set off for the golden land. In China, California was called *gam saan (gum shan)* "Gold Mountain" and it offered hope during desperate times to the people of southeast China.

The Guangdong (Canton) Province, with Guangzhou (Canton City) as its provincial capital, encompasses the Pearl River Delta region in southeast China. Facing the South China Sea, this region was exposed to the outside world through its rivers and coastal ports of Macao and Hong Kong. The majority of Chinese immigrants came from this subtropical region composed of twenty-four counties, many with local dialects that could not always be understood from one area to the other.

China is a great world power now, but its status was very different in the nineteenth century, a tumultuous period that saw the end of Qing Dynasty of Manchurian (Manchu) sovereigns who had ruled the majority Han Chinese for almost three hundred years (1644 to 1911). China, which called itself the Middle Kingdom, had been self-sufficient for thousands of years. Its emperors ruled under the Mandate of Heaven, adhering to a rigid social structure and unbending traditions that permeated throughout all levels of society. China prided itself on its high level of civilization; foreigners were unwelcome, considered to be barbarians. China's resistance to outside influences and change put it in a weak position to deflect incursions from the West and rebellion from within. Although there were efforts to modernize in the late nineteenth century, China was no match for aggression from Japan, Russia and European nations.

Just before the Gold Rush in the early 1840s, the area around Canton and north along the coast had been subjected to invasion from the British and other foreigners, who used illegal importation of opium as the means to gain a trade advantage in China. Although the Treaty of Nanjing in 1842 opened up five ports and ceded Hong Kong (now called Xianggang) to the British, there was official resistance to allowing westerners the right of trade and residence in Guangzhou. Still, despite strict regulations to prevent foreigners from having contact with the Chinese, news of gold in California reached the inhabitants of this coastal area, and once word spread, nothing could hold them back.

Many factors encouraged the wave of emigration from southeastern China. Poverty from overpopulation and paucity of land was exacerbated when the region was inundated with floods and consequent famine in 1846 to 1848. Clan warfare and local uprisings created fear, reprisals and destruction, worsened by the bloody Tai'ping Rebellion that raged for thirteen years, beginning in 1851. This was compounded by strife and warfare between two ethnically and linguistically distinct groups (Hakka and Punti), who settled the region during different periods. For peasant families struggling to survive under the most severe conditions, sending a father or son abroad to strike it rich or just to get work was a necessity. Merchants also saw opportunities for trade with other countries. Boatloads of Chinese set out for many regions of the world, including California.

It is estimated that seven out of ten Chinese who arrived in California in the nineteenth century came from four counties collectively known as the *Sze Yup* district, especially from the county of Toishan (formerly called Sunning). Having rocky, mountainous soil, Toishan, lacked enough arable land to sustain its burgeoning population; starvation was ever-present. The people from this area were primarily farmers and laborers. Another major influx of immigrants came from three counties collectively known as the *Sam Yup* district, which encompasses Guangzhou and had a more diverse and prosperous economy. Many of the immigrants from these counties were merchants and skilled craftsmen. The other area that contributed a significant number of immigrants was *Heungshan* (Xiangshan), now known as Chungshan (Zhongshan) on the south part of the Pearl River delta, where agriculture and fisheries dominated.

In 1852 approximately twenty thousand people from China came voluntarily to Gold Mountain. They arrived in San Francisco by steamship from Hong Kong after an arduous trip that lasted from forty-five days to more than three months. Money for the journey was sometimes lent by relatives and friends who pooled their funds. Most came by credit tickets in which Chinese merchant-brokers or regional district associations called *huiguans* extended credit to cover the thirty to fifty dollar passenger fee, to be repaid by the traveler from future earnings. Contrary to accusations of being forced "coolie labor," Chinese did not come to the United States by the contract labor system of forced servitude prevalent in Latin America and Southeast Asia.[1]

District associations were instrumental in providing a support system for Chinese people arriving to a strange country. They were well organized and highly effective, representing the Chinese in business and legal affairs. As new arrivals disembarked from the ship, they were greeted by kinsmen from their association (*huiguan*) who, recognizing the local dialect, conducted them to quarters in San Francisco, provided them with food and shelter, and equipped them with utensils and tools for the mines. A membership fee ensured contact with the association during their stay in the new world. Before a person could depart for China, the association issued a departure certificate recognized by shipping companies. If the person died in America, the association arranged to ship his bones back to China to reside in his ancestral home. The district associations cooperated for legal and protective purposes into a federation known in the U.S. as the Chinese Six Companies or Chinese Consolidated Benevolent Association, officially representing the different regions and dialects of the Guangdong Province to American governmental entities.

The social world in China could not have been more disparate than that of rough frontier California. With five thousand years of civilization, Chinese society was extremely disciplined and formalized; rules and laws defined every relationships and behavior. It was a country in which scholars, poets and philosophers were honored. Chinese society revolved around reverence for ancestors and close family ties. Traditions and an elaborate set of customs for birth, marriage and death prevailed.

Much of the focus of life was on the family and one's village, which consisted of members of the same clan, all with the same last name and related through common ancestors. The deeply imbedded Confucian ethical code stressed filial loyalty, the absolute respect and obedience of children to parents, and reverent loyalty to the emperor. Sons were expected to provide for their elderly parents; married daughters left their village to live in their husband's house, presided over by a sometimes tyrannical mother-in-law. The feet of many young girls were bound, small feet considered as a mark of beauty, but this practice also crippled women and kept them close to home. Pressures were great for them to give birth to sons. Husbands could take on second wives, and/or concubines, especially when the first wife failed to produce a son. An extended family of several generations often lived under the same roof, including

1 Chinese were kidnapped to labor as slaves on sugar plantations in Cuba and Peru. The pejorative label *coolie* was applied to laborers from India; in Chinese *kuli* means "bitterly hard" or "bitter labor."

grandparents, unmarried children, married sons and their families, and perhaps a widowed sister.

Most Chinese who came to California were men, many of whom were married. Marriage was extremely important because it meant the continuation of the family line. Wives usually stayed behind in China, rooted to their villages and their husband's family, discouraged from venturing abroad by tradition, economic circumstances, and the difficult life in the new world. Like many who flocked to California during the Gold Rush, most Chinese men did not initially intend to stay permanently. The responsibility to provide for the family remaining in China was a powerful incentive to work hard, make money and then return home.

The Chinese were often singled out as *sojourners*—people who came with no intention of settling long term in California or the United States. Certainly, this designation applied equally well to people of other nationalities who made the long journey with similar expectations of getting rich, providing for family back in their country of birth and returning home to live well. Alas, many who came to work in California labored under extreme hardship to just survive and save what they could to send back home. Arriving in California with high hopes, these Chinese immigrants encountered difficulties and hostility in the land of opportunity, yet they endured and persevered. A few even prospered. Some stayed permanently despite the obstacles that they encountered.

MINING AND BARRIERS TO THE SEARCH FOR GOLD

ARRIVAL

Most of the Chinese arriving in San Francisco set off with companions from their district to the mining regions. Rivers were the main conduit for reaching the foothills in the interior where placer mining was active. The Sacramento and San Joaquin rivers brought the newcomers on boats to the cities of Sacramento and Stockton, and from there they traveled by stage, pack horse or on foot towards camps in the northern or southern mining regions in the Sierra Nevada foothills. Amador County is generally considered part of the southern mining region, ranging from the Cosumnes River south to Mariposa County. Stockton was the major entry point to camps and towns in this part of the Sierra Nevada foothills, although the more northern towns of Fiddletown and Drytown could be reached by the road from Sacramento.

Groups of Chinese miners were spotted as early as 1851 near Drytown. These prospective miners frequently arrived in the new world with bedding, matting, clothing and sometimes utensils for preparing food. They carried their belongings and equipment in bags, boxes or baskets suspended at the end of a long bamboo pole slung across their shoulders. Most of the Chinese immigrants dressed in long blue quilted cotton tunics, loose blue trousers, and wide-brimmed triangular bamboo hats. Men shaved their heads at the crown except for a long braid called a queue, required as a sign of loyalty to the Qing dynasty that ruled China. Their appearance and strange language made them very conspicuous. Still, they had to adapt to the new environment. Thick wooden-soled shoes from China were replaced by heavy boots, much more practical for walking on muddy roads and wading in cold streams in search of gold.

Conversely, the appearance of Westerners must have been strange to Chinese, most of whom had not seen white people in China. In California, rough-looking men sporting ample beards would have seemed equally alien, in addition to women who were in public view and frequently independent, something unknown in cloistered China.

15

THE BUSINESS OF MINING

Chinese miners spread out along the rivers and creeks of Amador County, several men working together to dig, divert water, build dams, and sift through river rock and gravel to extract the precious grains of gold. Proceeds were shared among the workers, usually from the same clan or county organized into companies. Many of the Chinese coming from the Pearl River Delta were familiar with diverting water and constructing wing dams (long dams made of tree trunks stacked on top of one another) because of the floods that periodically inundated their region.

Both the Cosumnes and Mokelumne rivers had groups of Chinese working along their banks, as well as along the forks of Jackson Creek, Sutter Creek and other waterways. These miners were often relegated to mining claims abandoned by white miners or forced off claims if they successfully extracted gold. The Chinese worked with patience and perseverance. In October 1852 miner John Doble, later a resident of Volcano, reported that high waters on the Mokelumne River prevented mining companies from working there; yet persevering Chinese continued to mine on the bars of the river despite the rising water.

Several Chinese miners purchased and recorded mining claims from white Americans, evidence that Chinese did have legal mining rights. For example, Ah Koon & Company in 1855 purchased a mining claim from George Kreiss on a small gulch about one quarter of a mile from the town of Jackson; Ah Lot & Company in 1858 acquired a claim on the bed of the Mokelumne River from J. Donaldson; Ah On & Co., consisting of five Chinese from nearby Calaveras County, bought a claim in 1859 above the Big Bar Bridge on the Mokelumne River for the grand sum of $525 from W.F. Kearsing.[1]

The *Amador Ledger*'s traveling correspondent wrote in the weekly edition on August 15, 1857, "Here at Big Bar the Chinese have flumed the river for 700 yards and put in several wheels for pumping...I am informed that this year the river is pretty much owned by the Chinese."

Some transactions involved cooperation between the parties. In 1863, Louis Martell and company sold a mining claim on House Gulch at French Hill to Lang Fong & Company for $400. The agreement included the lower ditch and privilege of the dam on Italian Ranch as well as the upper ditch "when Martell does not want to use it" plus ten sluice boxes.

1 Amador County Deeds Grantor Index, 1854-1872, contain a few other examples of mining claims purchased by Chinese, including some purchased along the south fork of Jackson Creek.

However Martell reserved the right to discharge mine tailings through the tail race in the middle of the gulch. Louis Martell was a blacksmith from Jackson who later built *Martell's Station*, an inn, saloon, blacksmith and wagon shop at the junction of Jackson Gate and Sutter Creek roads, now off Highway 49 and known as Martell.

Chinese miners also gravitated to the Fiddletown area in the early 1850s, lured by tales of gold discoveries in the area. They spread out in the surrounding wooded hills, near farms and unpopulated areas, mining along Indian Creek and the north fork of Dry Creek. Water was as important as gold. Creeks flowed with water during the rainy months, occurring in winter and spring. Miners learned from experience about long stretches of dryness with no rainfall during the summer and early fall. Wooden flumes and ditches were built to convey water from the Cosumnes River

Figure 3. Chinese miners using the cradle. *Miner's Own Book, 1858*

ten miles southwest to the dry diggings around Fiddletown.

Chinese, along with other miners, drew water for mining from the Cosumnes Mining and Ditching Company's ditch or waterway. The company was purchased in 1860 by Columbus A. Purinton, a prominent resident of Fiddletown, who called himself a judge even though he had no formal position as such. He apparently had some control over the water in the north fork of Dry Creek around Fiddletown. He later became wealthy and powerful.

On the day before Christmas in 1859, an injunction was filed in the District Court against Purinton by five courageous Chinese residents of Fiddletown—Ah Owen, Ah Hop, Ah Sit, Ah Ye, and Ah Sow. They accused him of diverting water away from their mining claim on the north fork of Dry Creek, reducing the amount of water they could access for mining. The judge ordered the Chinese plaintiffs to put up a $300 bond for damages in the event that they lost the case. The trial went before a jury and several of Fiddletown's residents were summoned to appear on behalf of Purinton. Their testimony is lost, but a few months later the five Chinese plaintiffs had to pay $63 plus court and sheriff's fees. Apparently they had lost the case, possibly because they could not defend themselves in court. A California Supreme Court ruling in 1854 prohibited Chinese from testifying against whites.

Hostility to Chinese miners was common in the mining regions as competition for increasingly scarce placer gold became ever more intense. The journalist Alfred Doten mined throughout the foothills and commented in 1852 from Rich Gulch in Calaveras County, "There is considerable in the papers and much said about driving the Chinese out of the mines, except those who are willing to become naturalized citizens, as they are no benefit to the country at all, but rather a drain." [2]

The next year, white miners expressed resentment against the influx of Chinese miners above the Mokelumne River near Big Bar. An article in the September 12, 1853 *Daily Alta California* stated, "It is well known that the Chinese are willing to work for extremely low wages, and thus their labor comes into competition with that of American labor. The miners feel that this operates very hardly upon the newly arrived immigrants, many of whom have families to support..." They proposed a meeting to settle the issue and do what was deemed expedient.

California Governor Bigler, expressing alarm in April 1852 at "shipments of vast numbers of Coolies into this State," advocated new legislation to prevent or discourage Chinese from entering California. The eloquently written responses of the Chinese of San Francisco a month later talked about the repercussions:

> At many places they [the Chinese] have been driven away from their work and deprived of their claims, on which they had expended much

2 *The Journals of Alfred Doten*, 1849-1903, edited by Walter Van Tilberg Clark. Reno, Nevada, University of Nevada Press, 1973, pg. 111.

money and labor, and some of which they had bought from Americans at a high price…Many hundreds of Chinamen have thus been reduced to misery, and are now wandering about the mountains, looking for new places, where they my be allowed to dig, and fearful that they will be driven away again. All have suffered great losses, but we do not know how to describe the condition of those among them who had newly arrived, and had just expended all the money they had in getting to the mines.[3]

Conflict between Chinese and Americans was especially apparent in mining areas in counties to the south. In 1852, miners in the town of Columbia in Tuolumne County voted to bar Chinese from the mines. Near the town of Angels Camp in Calaveras County, American miners in 1857 gave the Chinese six months to leave that mining district. They resolved that any white miner who sold a claim to Chinese or employed Chinese workers should forfeit his interest in mining claims. Neighboring counties were invited to act similarly.[4]

In Amador County's Drytown, Chinese miners came under threat when white miners there held a meeting in December 1856 aimed at expelling Chinese from their mining district. By a close vote of twenty-three to twenty, it was decided that the Chinese must depart by the following month. However, not all agreed to expel the Chinese, and another meeting was called a few days later to rescind the resolution. According to the local *Volcano Weekly Ledger* of December 20, 1856, "The citizens of Drytown are in favor of letting the Chinamen remain." And so they did.

FOREIGN MINERS' TAX

The Chinese were permitted by the State Legislature to continue immigrating to California, but in 1852 it re-imposed the previously suspended Foreign Miners' Tax at $3 per month. The Legislature raised the tax to $4 per month the next year and later amended it to apply exclusively to Chinese. It continued to raise the tax until, after reaching a high of $6 per month in 1856, local merchants complained that they were losing a lucrative business when Chinese started to leave the mining area. Chinese were good customers of American businesses and always paid their bills on time. The tax was then lowered to $4 per month, half

3 *An Analysis of the Chinese Question consisting of a Special Message of the Governor, and, in Reply Thereto, Two Letters of the Chinamen, and a Memorial of the Citizens of San Francisco.* San Francisco, *San Francisco Herald*, 1852.
4 *Evening Bulletin*, San Francisco, November 19, 1857.

of which went to counties. From 1854 to 1870 Amador County garnered $137,019 from its Chinese miners.

Amador County made it particularly inviting for collectors of the Foreign Miners' Tax by upping the incentives. At the end of 1854, the Board of Supervisors awarded collectors a commission of 15 percent, which it raised five months later to 25 percent, the board deeming the 15 percent specified by law "insufficient for such services." The tax imposed an onerous burden on Chinese miners and many hid from officials when tax collectors and other officials came around. Some collectors abused their authority. The *Sacramento Bee* reported an incident at the Upper Crossing of the Cosumnes River on February 23, 1858:

> Today the Chinamen of the vicinity were visited by the officers who collect the monthly mining tax. The Chinamen were treated in the most brutal manner by these gentry. In the Absence of white men to witness the proceeding, they beat some of the Chinamen most unmercifully with a whip. I saw one man whose back was beaten almost of a jelly by these courageous servants of the people. It is high time that some measures were adopted to put a stop to such unmanly and dastardly conduct towards unresisting persons as Chinamen. Chinamen do not appear to have adequate protection from the assaults of persons who usually discharge the duties of foreign miners' tax collector.

The monthly Foreign Miners' Tax greatly affected the livelihood and security of Chinese immigrants. Nonetheless, sufficient tax was collected from Chinese miners to contribute half of the total tax revenue for the State of California during a twenty year period. The tax was declared unconstitutional in 1870.

OTHER ENDEAVORS

Road building employed many laborers, as trails needed to be widened into roads for wagons, stage lines and commerce between towns and cities. Chinese were prominent among the laborers constructing roads throughout the growing county. A Road Overseer's report for September 1855 regarding building a bridge in Fiddletown documented that whites were paid $3 per day, Chinese $2. The Chinese as well as other residents of Amador County were forced to pay a quarterly road poll tax, essentially a head tax levied upon all males between ages twenty and fifty years. The tax amounted to $2 per quarter, an entire day's pay for Chinese laborers. So many Chinese were involved in road building that they were most likely easy targets for the poll tax. Two hundred Chinese people paid the poll tax according to an April 1864 Road Overseer's report. Other reports document that whites along with Chinese paid the tax. This unpopular tax was in place in California until 1914.

Working hard for little compensation, Chinese laborers helped build the roads, bridges, ditches, and canals throughout the county, often working in large companies overseen by Chinese labor bosses who provided food and shelter to the workers.

THE GRISWOLD MURDER, CRIME AND JUSTICE

Although Chinese could not testify against whites in court, they were still involved with the law whether seeking redress from grievances or accused of crime. Assistance in court came from Chinese interpreters fluent in English or in some cases, Americans fluent in speaking Cantonese. Chinese miners and members of their community were generally law-abiding, but some resorted to crime.

THE GRISWOLD MURDER

A sensational crime occurred near Jackson on November 7, 1857, that put additional pressure on vulnerable Chinese communities. A respected man named Martin Van Buren Griswold was brutally murdered, his body hidden under the bed of the Chinese cook who occupied the same

Figure 4. News headlines. *Volcano Weekly Ledger*

quarters. Van Buren Griswold was the confidential manager of a wealthy man, Horace Kilham, who owned orchards, bought and sold gold dust, and collected rent for use of water rights on his ditch. Five Chinese men, including the cook were accused of the crime. Four of these men were convicted, ostensibly "the first Chinamen who have ever been convicted, in a civilized country, of the murder of a white man." The murder and hunt for the perpetrators were highly publicized and sensationalized in the local press and newspapers throughout Northern California.

The cook, Fou Sin, lived in a cabin with Griswold and Kilham in an area of intensive mining activity, close to a trail leading to the town of Jackson. When Griswold's strangled and bludgeoned body was discovered the day after his murder, suspicion fell on Fou Sin and his friend Chou Yee as well as two other "shabbily and roughly dressed" Chinese who were seen outside the cabin on the morning of the murder. The key to the safe and its contents, estimated at a value of $2,000 to $5000 were missing. Fou Sin, Chou Yee, and the other men were already on the run.

This incident reveals some interesting information about Chinese communities. First of all, they were widespread. Fou Sin and Chou Yee travelled north, going from Sacramento to Auburn to Oroville to Marysville, where they were finally apprehended. All of these places had Chinese sections, although the fugitives didn't necessarily stay there. The two men were always able to find work, whether mining or in a laundry or in a Chinese store. The other factor was that Chinese communities in Amador County and elsewhere assisted in the arrest of the suspects, though somewhat under duress. The *Volcano Weekly Ledger* of November 14 warned:

> We would not distrust the Chinamen, nor threaten them; but they should
> be given to know in a manner not to be misunderstood, that *no excuse*
> will be taken. They CAN produce the murderers—THEY MUST DO
> IT, or fearful indeed will be the vengeance visited upon the Chinese
> people in California. It is the first murder committed by Chinamen in
> the State, and the entire white population are deeply interested in its
> speedy punishment. The Chinese murderers at home are the most cruel,
> heartless and abandoned on the face of the earth; they have been kept
> down in California through fear, and a consciousness of the superiority
> of the whites; let them be induced to think otherwise, and no man's life
> will have the least security.

With the prospect of violent repercussions, the Chinese fully cooperated, both monetarily and in the search for the accused. Reward money was raised—$500 from the Chinese residents of Jackson, $500 from the Governor, $1,000 from Kilham with an additional $500 for recovery of the lost items. The San Francisco *Evening Bulletin* reported that the merchants of that city, represented by the Chinese Six Companies, were considering offering a large reward as well. The Chief of Police had "represented to them the disadvantages under which the Chinese population would labor if the murderers were suffered to escape, and particularly if it were finally ascertained that they had been harbored in this city." A few days later, the *Volcano Weekly Ledger* of November 21 stated that the Chinese Six Companies had offered even more money, $1,500 for the arrest of Fou Sin, and $800 each for two of the other named accomplices, Chou Yee and Coon See. The reward money now totaled $5,100 for capturing the alleged murderers.

The arrest of the suspects could not have been achieved without assistance from California's Chinese immigrants. By the end of November, the Chinese from Amador County had apprehended Cheung Quoon Yow (referred to as Coon You). On December 4, the Chinese residents of Jackson had apprehended and arrested another suspect, Coon See, in Chinese Camp, Tuolumne County to the south. Fou Sin and Chou Yee were arrested at the end of December in Marysville, betrayed by a former friend who may have been after the reward money. Ah Hung, from Indian Creek near the Shenandoah Valley, was the fifth suspect to be caught. He was apprehended by the Sheriff during the first week of January in Fiddletown, perhaps sheltered by its Chinese community. He was later acquitted because of lack of evidence.

Fou Sin and Chou Yee were tried separately on February 25, 1858. The other two men, Coon You and Coon See were tried the following day. The men were defended by R.M. Briggs, a notable attorney in the area; an interpreter was also retained, a man working for the City of San Francisco, Charles T. Carvalho, who had lived in China for years. An all-white male jury tried the case; women could neither serve on a jury nor testify. The accused men did not testify, although three Chinese men were called as witnesses by the defense in the second trial. Each trial was concluded in a single day.

After a short time deliberating, the jury judged Fou Sin and Chou Yee to be guilty of murder in the first degree. The trial of Coon You and Coon See, who were from a different district of Guangdong, was not as conclusive, hinging on whether white witnesses recognized them and could distinguish one Chinese person from another. Coon You was found guilty. Coon See was found not guilty, but he was retained in custody to be retried for a lesser offense. A few days later, he was tried and found guilty of grand larceny for robbing the house. Despite the lesser charge for Coon See, all four men were sentenced to be hung on April 16. He escaped the shame of public hanging by committing suicide in jail a week before the sentence was to be carried out.

Following the capture and trial, Thomas Springer, the publisher of the *Amador Ledger*, issued a pamphlet, *Murder of M.V. B. Griswold by Five Chinese Assassins.*[1] Although it contributed to the sensationalism of the case, this pamphlet is of particular interest because it contains the words of the convicted men, providing details of their lives, their versions of the crime and final wishes.

Fou Sin described his life before he came to Jackson, which gives insight into his restless spirit and both his opportunities and difficulties in finding work. His account is lucid and highly specific, including names of ships, their captains, dates and names of places he traveled to. Born in Guangdong Province as the son of a farmer and stonecutter, he had served on various ships since he was fourteen years old, stopping in ports in Hong Kong, England, Singapore, Japan, Hawaii, Massachusetts and Russia. He was a cabin boy on English and American ships and stayed in Singapore for three years as a British officer's "boy," where he learned English. In the Sandwich Islands (Hawaii), he was involved in whaling and obtaining provisions for a French ship. Fou Sin stayed in Honolulu for almost two years working as a cook for a wholesale merchant who "had a wife and children, and I got along first rate." Then in early 1856, he signed up as a ship's steward for a schooner serving the Islands. Six months later, as second steward, he boarded an American steamship that was being delivered to the Russian government (its purchaser) at Russia's far eastern border with China. From there he sailed on a Russian a man-of-war that first delivered provisions to soldiers and then, "Taking in ballast, we sailed for San Francisco, where we arrived after a voyage of some three months and a half, on New Year's Day, 1857. I was never in California previous to that time."

In California his luck turned prior to getting the job in Jackson. Many Chinese had the capability of being excellent cooks, a mainstay of

1 *Murder of M.V.B. Griswold by Five Chinese Assassins.* Jackson, T.A. Springer & Company, 1858. A copy is held at the Amador County Archives from the original at Henry E. Huntington Library. Quotations from Fou Sin are from the pamphlet.

employment for men in need of work. Fou Sin was in and out of work in San Francisco, always hired as a cook, a few times in boarding houses and hotels operated by black men. He stated in the pamphlet that when he was unemployed "for two months after[wards] I was about the city with nothing to do, and slept and eat [sic] in a Chinese barber shop. Then I got into a scrape at a Spanish dance house on Pacific Street." He related getting into an argument there with a "drunken Negro" who started cursing him and moved towards him "as though he was going to fight with me. I pulled out my knife and told him, 'G-d d—[God damn] you, I'll cut your throat.'" Fou Sin dropped the knife when an officer intervened. He was subsequently arrested and spent two months in jail. Upon his release, he was briefly hired as the third cook on a steamer, then in another job change, he was employed for six weeks cooking for a San Francisco hotel. Again, he was unemployed for several weeks. During this period, he got into another fight in a Chinese brothel. Several were injured and arrested but this time he escaped. His meeting with Chou Yee and relocation to Jackson could be interpreted as fortuitous or fateful.

Fou Sin had developed a friendship with Chou Yee in Hawaii and encountered him again when he first landed in San Francisco. Chou Yee worked for three months in the California Hotel in San Francisco, afterwards gravitating to Stockton and from there to Chinese Camp, where he worked as a cook for four months. He, too, moved around, eventually coming to Jackson. Currently employed as a cook at the Q Ranch in Ione, Chou Yee convinced Fou Sin, out of work and out of money, to accompany him to Jackson where there were cooking opportunities in the foothills. A few weeks later, Fou Sin obtained a job cooking for Horace Kilham and Martin Van Buren Griswold.

As with all crimes, it is difficult to separate truth from lies; inconsistencies abound, recollections differ, and contesting versions are given. From the finger-pointing accounts of Fou Sin, Chou Yee and Coon You published in the pamphlet plus the evidence produced at the trial, it seems clear that the men were deeply involved in some or all aspects of the crime. What we see here, especially with Fou Sin and Chou Yee, is restless men, moving from place to place, seeking change, drifting from job to job, getting into trouble, visiting gambling houses and brothels. Certainly, this profile matches that of many adventurers who came to California seeking gold and wealth, some of whom resorted to committing a crime to get rich without hard work. There were scoundrels and dishonest people among the Chinese, just as with other nationalities.

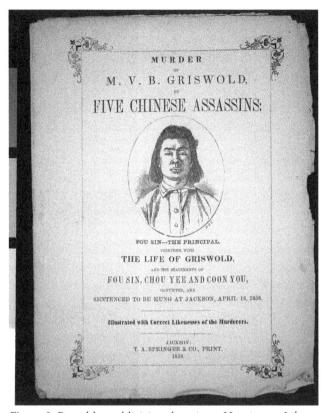

Figure 5. Pamphlet publicizing the crime. *Huntington Library*

The pamphlet included the translation of a letter and epitaph written by Fou Sin to his father and brother.[2] Imbued with Confucian philosophy and filial devotion, his words reveal a very different mind-set from that of the West. As the eldest son, Fou Sin had the responsibility of caring for his family. Now the burden fell on his younger brother to whom he advised, "When you become a man, be not wild, nor frivolous, nor fond of wild plays. Let your words be trust. Avoid idle talk. On you is now centered the affection, so complete, of a whole house. Whilst this I say, you are my brother to all time."

Fou Sin had expressed hope that his brother and father would send for his bones to be taken back to China for burial, a wish shared by all Chinese

2   Fou Sin's letter was enclosed in a sealed inner envelope, yet it was "deemed proper [by the court] to open it and have it translated, for obvious reasons." The epitaphs of the other men were added to the letter and translated, also by Charles Carvalho. The original was to be "duly forwarded" to Fou Sin's father and brother, enclosed in the original outer envelope directed to the Man Lee Store in San Francisco.

immigrants. "I have seen many people buried at sea; their bones cannot be sent back, and white men in California allow theirs to rest where they are buried. But I would a little rather they would send and take me back to the Flowery Kingdom [China]; I hope and think they will. Then hath the spirit peace forever." Knowing that this would probably not be the case, he asked that nine fingernails be sent to his family in a box with the letters, two gold pieces worth five dollars, and his epitaph. He was only twenty-six years old.

For his epitaph, he wrote:
Green spring, I await you in gladness
Who can obstruct or impede the vast harvest of the grain?
True felicity must come from self, otherwise 'tis nothing.
After joyful spring, comes tedious autumn.

The three other men also wrote poetic epitaphs. From Chou Yee, "My body hath gone before me, borne on clouds. My youth was coupled with twenty springs; I was unconscious of it, but thus it was. I loved to follow the bridegroom of the Southern Hills."

Alas, Fou Sin, Chou Yee and Coon You were executed April 16, 1858 on specially constructed gallows before a crowd that numbered close to five thousand in an atmosphere that could only be called riotous, with drinking, gambling, fights and injuries. The pamphlet on the crime was published by Springer about ten days before the execution and distributed free to the crowd as a souvenir; later it was sold for fifty cents. The *Weekly Alta California related* on April 24, "We were exceedingly grieved to see a large number of women present at the execution. We observed but few Chinamen present at the scene at the death of their three countrymen." Fou Sin, Chou Yee, and Coon You were buried in Jackson at the foot of the gallows, far from their homeland.

Even Horace Kilham was deeply affected—his property was put up for sale in February and soon after the trial, he sold his orchards and water ditches, and moved away from Amador County

Anti-Chinese sentiments and racism played a large role in sensationalizing this case and in putting great pressure on Chinese communities to cooperate or face serious consequences such as enacting "laws that will drive Chinese from the mines and from the State." It cannot be overlooked that most Chinese were honest and hardworking, and willingly helped officials capture the suspects.

OTHER COURT CASES

Several of the cases in the 1860s tried in local township courts involved Chinese men accused of petty (petit) larceny. Those found guilty were ordered to pay fines of forty dollars or more, or spend time in jail. Some fines were as high as $100 or $200. Most spent time in jail because they could not put up the money. In March 1865 several Chinese in the Drytown area were accused on separate charges of this crime and pled not guilty. One man, Ah Cun, was found guilty. However, he appealed his case to a higher court and it was dismissed. Of four other people accused of petty larceny, three were dismissed and the fourth paid the fine. Other cases tried in Jackson followed a similar pattern; several were dismissed, some for lack of evidence, others found guilty and fined.

Two men accused of assault and battery, Ah Hing and Ah Quan, were tried by jury in September 1865. The first jury of twelve could not agree on a verdict. A second jury was called to try the case. This jury found the defendants not guilty and both men were acquitted. A Chinese language interpreter was present in both trials.

Judicial decisions in Amador County did not necessarily show prejudice against the Chinese, especially those who were victims of crime. On October 15, 1864, a man named Samuel Baker was tried three separate times for robbing Chinese people. In the first case, he was sentenced to five years in state prison for robbing Ah Yun and Ah Wy of eighty dollars, including gold dust worth fifty dollars. In the second case, he stripped Ah King of everything on his body—not only gold and silver coins, but a pistol, a silver watch and chain, trousers, hat, shirt, two pair of underwear and a handkerchief. Two Chinese men were called as witnesses and Baker was sentenced to an additional two years in prison. The third case involved the robbery of Ah Man Wo for his pistol, a black hat and a seventy-five dollar package of gold dust. Two more years were added to Baker's sentence, making a total of seven years in state prison. It is interesting that two of the victims were armed with a pistol; both were robbed on the same day.

In other court cases, Chinese accused of burglary were prosecuted for their crime. Ah Fat, pled guilty of entering a storehouse with the intent to steal gold dust as well as gold and silver coins. He was sentenced on October 14, 1865 to one year in state prison. The same day Ah Sam, accused of entering a house with intent to steal clothing, provisions, and bedding, also pled guilty and was sentenced to two years in state prison.

In a similar case the following year, Ah Kee (also known as Ah Sam) was sentenced to one year in state prison for breaking and entering a house in Drytown to steal clothing and goods. It seems like there was not much distinction between intent and accomplishing the crime.

The Chinese also settled conflicts among themselves in the courts. Some clashes were caused by personal quarrels, perhaps between people from different companies or districts; others were the result of criminal activity. For example, on January 12, 1865, Wo Ho was sentenced to two years in state prison for robbing Ah Hoy of gold and silver pieces worth $220. Another case involved a brawl that occurred in Jackson on September 1, 1875 over a two dollar debt. It started as street fight between a miner known as Ah Vhan (Ah On) and Ah Chow (also referred to as Ah Chew). The fight was broken up by an American man. It continued in Ah Vhan's room when Ah Chew allegedly kicked in the locked door and wounded Ah Vhan in the abdomen and thigh with an eight-inch knife. The room was described as dark, about nine feet long and six feet wide— small quarters in a boarding house. Several Chinese witnesses were called, including Ah Vhan's wife, who claimed to be present in the room when the knifing occurred. Some acquaintances of Ah Chew testified that he was leaving for home in Sutter Creek rather than fleeing from the crime. The testimony was conflicting and confusing, including failure of the arresting officer to notice if there was blood on Ah Chew's clothes. Nonetheless, Ah Chew was found guilty by the Justice of the Peace.

In other conflicts among Chinese, they could call upon their district associations to dispense justice internally without resorting to the courts. District associations also provided assistance when members needed legal support or English translation in the courtroom. For example, Ken Kwong, who did not speak English, sought the help of his district association in a Grand Jury hearing where he was the only witness. The association sent a translator of Cantonese from San Francisco who could interpret Kwong's testimony. This prompted the defense attorney for the accused man, Charles Merchand, to obtain for the defense a person also familiar with the Cantonese language.

The case involved the murder of Kwong's partner during an invasion of their cabin by six armed men in October 1881. The two Chinese men barely made a living from mining and maintaining a small garden near the Mokelumne River and had been accused by some whites of stealing cattle. At the hearing, the newspaper reporter from the *Amador Ledger* concluded that Kwong's testimony was credible and faulted the Grand

Jury for discharging Merchand after only one hour of deliberation. He wrote, "Justice cuts some peculiar pranks occasionally....Perhaps it would not be out of place for the Grand Jury next month to look into the transaction again." Clearly, this was a situation where a white murder suspect of a Chinese man was let go, precluding an indictment and trial.

Overall the administration of justice to Chinese immigrants in Amador County was erratic, ranging from fairness to discrimination with penalties of large fines and long prison sentences for minor crimes and worse, unfairly favoring whites over Chinese.

THE RISE OF AMADOR COUNTY CHINATOWNS

Although life was precarious, Chinese in Amador County continued to mine and live in towns and mining camps. Chinese neighborhoods, or Chinatowns, became a visible part of growing towns, all connected with gold discoveries nearby. Like many immigrant groups, the Chinese lived clustered together where they could socialize and do business with people who spoke their language. In these communities, the Chinese retained their customs, obtained merchandise, provided services and traded with each other as well as with neighboring Europeans and Americans. Chinese sections were located in areas of commercial activity, usually along the main street of a town. They were close to the centers of trade yet segregated because of their ethnicity and race.

The largest Chinatowns in Amador County were established in Drytown, Jackson, Ione, and Fiddletown. Volcano and Lancha Plana encompassed Chinatowns as well. The towns with the fewest Chinese residents—Amador City, Sutter Creek and Plymouth—tended to be the most vocal when it came to anti-Chinese sentiments.

The assessment poll from 1856 lists Chinese with taxable assets in Jackson, Drytown, and Fiddletown. Hom-Zen in Jackson was identified as a "doctor, barber, and tailor," an interesting combination of skills that entail cutting and stitching. In Drytown, two property owners kept a "China store." Early deeds in the 1860s primarily cover these towns and show that enterprising Chinese bought property from white owners and also sold property to whites and to each other. The Chinese entrepreneurial spirit, where material wealth is prized, encourages investment in property as a sign of prosperity.

Most recorded transactions took place in Jackson, the county seat. Around Jackson, three Chinese settlements arose by the early 1850s, all close to Jackson Creek. One was near the south fork of Jackson Creek, south of the town. Another was in an active mining area along the north fork of Jackson Creek called The Gate, a village leading to the town of Jackson. There a man named Ah Chut owned two acres. He planted a garden on one acre which he sold in December 1862 to Augustine Chichizola, an Italian who established a store in the area. The other one-acre parcel was sold to Ah Ping, who paid $173 for the purchase; Chichizola bought the garden property for less, $150.

In the town of Jackson proper, Chinese congregated at the north end of Main Street, along both sides of the north fork of Jackson Creek, purchasing and renting parcels in the busy commercial section. Initially, the neighborhoods were not totally segregated into Chinese and European-American, though certainly Chinese predominated in this part of town.

The Drytown township in 1860 was almost half Chinese (44 percent). Chinese individuals either purchased or rented property in what became the Chinese section of town from a family that owned many lots in Drytown.[1]

Figure 6. Fiddletown Chinese buildings ca.1990. *D. Zorbas*

The early Chinatowns of both Jackson and Drytown were consumed by fire. A catastrophic fire in Jackson on August 23, 1862 destroyed the entire commercial and residential section of the town, including one hundred Chinese houses valued at a total of $50,000. In 1867 the Chinese part of Drytown was destroyed by fire. Over forty Chinese buildings were burned, "most of them of little value," according to the newspaper. The principal loss was to several Chinese merchants. However, persevering

1   Tordoff, Judith D. "Test Excavations at the Block 8 Site, Ca-Ama-305/H Locus A, Drytown, Amador County, California," The Hornet Foundation of California State University, Sacramento, California for the California Department of Transportation, February, 1987. The report contains more information on Drytown Chinese based on archeological excavations and historical research.

Chinese residents were not deterred and rebuilt stores and living quarters in both towns.

In Ione and Lancha Plana, Chinese composed 24 percent of the total population in 1860, developing Chinese sections in both towns.

Of the various Chinatowns in Amador County, little remains—a store in Volcano, a store in Plymouth, both occupied but not built by Chinese, a sign written in Chinese uncovered beneath a ceiling in Jackson, a road called China Graveyard Road in Jackson Gate, a variety of objects from Chinese daily life exhibited in the Amador County Museum, and a monument in Ione where its Chinatown once stood. Fiddletown is the exception. It has more structures remaining from an early Chinatown than any other community in Amador County, or for that matter, in any California mining town. All were built in the mid-1850s or early 1860s—the Chew Kee Store, the Chinese Gambling House opposite, the Chinese General Store to the east as well as an adobe building on a hill, use unknown and privately owned. Furthermore, the Chew Kee Store survived with furnishings and artifacts intact until its last Chinese inhabitant died in 1965. And equally important, its written papers have been preserved, many of those in Chinese now translated.

THE FIDDLETOWN CHINESE COMMUNITY DEVELOPS

Fiddletown started out as a mining camp in 1849 during the height of the Gold Rush, attracting miners from many parts of the world. According to legend, it was settled initially by a group of miners from Missouri, who played the fiddle during slow times when there was no water in the creeks for mining—hence the melodious name Fiddletown.

Fiddletown parallels the curves of the north fork of Dry Creek, located along a narrow pass with steep wooded hills on the south side. It ascends the foothills at 1,687 feet, which placed it near other hilly mining camps and rich diggings to east and the south. The town started to grow in 1852 after gold discoveries in nearby terrain enticed miners and merchants into the area. This was also the year that thousands of Chinese arrived in California to try their luck with mining.

Fiddletown developed an active commercial center in and around east Main Street, evolving into a trading center that supplied residents, farms and mining camps in the vicinity. A new resident in 1853 described a thriving business section: fifteen to twenty stores, four hotels and taverns, a couple of bakeries, two or three restaurants, three blacksmith shops, and a carpenter shop. In addition, there were dance halls, gambling places, and even a public bath. The establishment of a school, a Methodist Church

Figure 7. Fiddletown East Main Street, 1856. *Amador County Archives*

and a post office gave the town the bare essentials of legitimacy. At its peak in the mid-1850s, Fiddletown had around two thousand people.

FIDDLETOWN CHINATOWN

In 1855, an American merchant named Spencer Richards bought a store that catered to the Chinese. Fiddletown already had a sizable Chinese population by then. At least half of his customers were Chinese, and he employed a Chinese clerk. Spencer wrote to a friend:

> The place that I am located in now is quite a little town, some six or eight stores, four public houses, four stages leave every day, but I can't say that I like the place very much, to [sic] many Chinamen. I am down on them although they are the best customers that I have, I keep a regular assortment of China goods, very good profit on China goods but the profits are small for what they used to be in Cal[ifornia][1]...

By the end of that decade, Chinese residents of Fiddletown formed their own neighborhood and commercial section where they could live and buy the food, clothing, utensils and objects essential to maintaining their culture. Not speaking English and far from their families, they could gather together in the Chinese section. Many may have been from the same district in southeast China, speaking the same dialect, hoping to get rich in Gold Mountain. Word of opportunities in California had spread throughout the province of Guangdong, enticing relatives, clan members and the adventurous to join those who had made the long voyage.

Most of the Chinese settled on the west side of Fiddletown along both sides of Main Street, close to the town's entrance and the sprawling Union Hotel—a curious location given that Chinatowns were usually poor and crowded. It is probable that the hotel was constructed early in the life of the town and that whites inhabited this vicinity before the Chinese section developed.

A stagecoach passenger arriving in Fiddletown would first see the large two-story hotel. After making a stop to let passengers on and off, the coach would head east and pass by a cluster of Chinese wooden houses and stores. No photograph of the Chinese section remains, but the structures must have been flimsy, wooden, and close together. The town's watchman in 1858 feared that this part of town could go up in flames and counseled "each habitation to provide casks of water, in a position to be

---

1 Spencer Richard's Letter to his friend Warren, Fiddletown, June 26, 1855(?), Bancroft Library, University of California, Berkeley, BANC MSS C-B 547:26

speedily used in case of fire."[2] On the other hand, most of the buildings in the American and European commercial part of Fiddletown were also constructed of wood, although more permanent brick buildings had started to appear.

Main Street Chinatown included Chinese merchandise stores and groceries, the herb store, gambling houses, brothels, restaurants, residences and boarding houses. Merchants, miners, laborers, gamblers, butchers, boarding house operators and packers for stores lived in the community. Six "women of pleasure" resided together in the same quarters with groups of gamblers next door. The town was small enough so that there was ample interaction between the Chinese, European and American residents in regards to services and trade. Fiddletown had a diverse population with people from every state and many countries of the world in addition to the Miwuk Native Americans and the Mexicans who were first in the area.

By 1860 close to a third of the population in the greater Fiddletown area was Chinese. According to the U.S. Census of Population, the total population was about 1,100 of which 295 were Chinese. Many Chinese may not have been counted, given the language barrier, Foreign Miners' Tax and the overall avoidance of government officials, a practice already developed in China where taxation was oppressive. Fiddletown's Chinese population was never second to that of San Francisco as has been proclaimed in oral and some written accounts.[3] Compared to the 2,719 in San Francisco in 1860, a total of 2,568 Chinese resided in the entire Amador County. The numbers of Chinese in Fiddletown have been exaggerated, but not their importance. The Chinese were a major constituent of the town's workers and residents for several decades.

The majority (86 percent) of the Chinese people listed in the 1860 Census were miners, scattered in camps and living in contiguous groups of five to seven men near creeks or promising diggings close to Fiddletown and the nearby Shenandoah Valley. They remain anonymous, first names listed for the most part as "Ah." Only their ages distinguish them, ranging from eighteen to fifty-two years, with most in their twenties and thirties, living far from home.

A few stand out because of their occupations: Ah Chum and Ah Lum, merchants; Ah Tung and Ah Lon, storekeepers; Ah Young and Ah Han, butchers; Ah Chee, Ah King and Ah Jack, boarding house operators; Le

2 *Amador Weekly Ledger*, June 5, 1858.
3 The assertion that Fiddletown once had 5,000 Chinese, repeated in many sources, does not correlate with actual records.

Lang and Ah Moke merchants; Ah Sing, gardener; Ah Poo and Ah Quan washer men; Chi Wing, cook. What were their full names? What were their lives like? So much was never recorded.

The Chinese in Fiddletown were fortunate because they found an advocate in Constable Stephen Davis, who became their spokesman and friend. Originally from Wales, Davis came west with a wagon train between 1851 and 1852, serving as a scout and interpreter. A remarkable man, he apparently could learn a new language in a few weeks, and spoke six Chinese dialects as well as several Native American languages. Davis helped Fiddletown's Chinese by serving as their interpreter and writing mining claims for them. What a boon this must have been to people unable to transact business in English! Unfortunately, Davis was accidentally killed on April 3, 1868, when he reached down into a barrel in the Fiddletown General Store and the gun on his belt went off. Left behind was his pregnant wife, Mary Kane Davis. Later, when her baby son, Stephen Kane Davis, was a few months old, "Chinese men came to her house, took the baby, and in a parade, carried him up and down the main street to honor the man who had befriended them." Mary later told her son that even though she was alone, she felt watched over.[4]

Figure 8. Union Hotel at west entry. *Amador County Archives*

4 Cowan, Mary Davis and Jack Lawrence, "Memories of our Grandmother," typescript.

CHINATOWN PROPERTY OWNERS AND RENTERS

A few Chinese residents purchased property on Main Street, contrary to the common belief that Chinese could not own land. Assessment records from 1856 list Long [Lang], Neon, Ah Dan Che-on, and Chew as owning property. However, most Chinese were renters, beholden to American owners who bought up property in the Chinese section, renting to Chinese there and in other parts of town.

In June 1855, Fiddletown resident Meyer Raphael filed a formal complaint to the Justice of the Peace against his tenant, a Chinese man referred to as "Ah Poon, alias" who rented a house on north Main Street between Raphael's storehouse and a saloon. Rent was set at thirty dollars a month, payable in advance for a period four months, January to April. Yet after May arrived, Ah Poon lingered in the house without paying rent and refused to leave the premises, hence the reason for Raphael's complaint. On May 14 Justice of the Peace E.R. Yates ordered the Sheriff to summons Ah Poon to come before him. A few days later, Raphael asked for the case to be transferred to another court, averring that he could not have a fair or impartial trial before Yates. It is unlikely that Justice E.R. Yates, a Southerner, would favor the Chinese defendant, but he might have had a personal grudge against Raphael.

The Chinese occupancy of west Main Street is revealed in early deeds and other documents. Partners William Ray and John Doss owned six houses "occupied by Chinamen" between the Union Hotel and the Gist & Forsythe Livery Stable to the east. One of the properties acquired in 1859 was next to "a lot owned by a Chinamen named Lang."

Property on west Main Street owned by Ray changed hands after he died, first to his widow Elizabeth Ray who sold five houses to his former partner John Doss in 1865. The following year Doss sold four houses and lots to D.M. Goff who already owned a few adjoining parcels. The various houses had adjacent Chinese neighbors: businesses Ah Moke & Co., Ah Low & Co., Lang & Co. and Wo Sing. In 1866, the Sing Lee Co., consisting of three partners, sold one of its parcels to Goff, retaining an adjoining lot to the west.

Goff was an influential person in Fiddletown and in the county. He was a well-off livestock dealer, possessing real estate worth $1,500 in 1860. From 1867 through 1869, he served as Amador County Supervisor, an elected position. Goff and another resident of Fiddletown, W.T. Gist owned most of Fiddletown's Chinatown. Goff died in April, 1870 and his widow Mary took over as property owner.

W.T. Gist had been elected Constable in 1854 and 1855, acting as Deputy Sheriff. He and two other men were responsible for collecting the Foreign Miners' Tax from Fiddletown's Chinese population. Somehow they managed to inexplicably lose forty-five licenses for taxes collected in June 1860, which were to be handed over to the Amador County Sheriff. Five years later, an attachment was put on property owned by Gist because of $400 overdue principal and interest on a loan. His property included four houses occupied by Chinese on the north side of west Main Street.

It is possible that either Gist or Goff built the two-story brick building that became the Foo Kee General Store. Gist made substantial improvements to town lots amounting to $2,000 in 1855 and $1,200 in 1856. Goff also made early improvements on property and afterward owned the two adjoining lots. No mention is made in these early records of the rammed-earth Chew Kee Store, later referred to as the 'Dobe [adobe] and no deeds were recorded. When it was built remains a mystery. One historian postulated that the Chew Kee Store could have been constructed around 1860, not in the mid-50s as is generally estimated.[5]

---

5 Cenotto, Larry, "Some Fiddletown Buildings," in *Logan's Alley*, vol. 5, pgs. 194-197. After examining Fiddletown deeds, Cenotto speculated that the Chew Kee Store may have been built around 1860 and that the buildings that became the Chinese gambling house and Foo Kee General Store were built by Caucasians in the 1850s.

FIDDLETOWN'S CHINESE HERB DOCTOR: YEE FUNG CHEUNG

Dr. Yee Fung Cheung was the first known occupant to live and work in the rammed earth building now known as the Chew Kee Store. It was constructed by Chinese workers using an ancient technique of packing (i.e., ramming) earth mixed with water and straw between removable wooden forms, resulting in walls about two feet thick. This technique was used in building the Great Wall of China as well as other walls and houses in China. Yet the style of the structure is unique, adapted to the California environment. The steep roof is made of wooden shingles, and the interior paneling, shelves and cabinets are wood, once plentiful from surrounding forests. The overhang on the front porch shelters the entry from pelting rain and the intense sun of summer in the foothills. The front commercial part of the store has a larger area than is typical in a Chinese herb store, providing a more flexible use of space where people could gather. The building faces south, an auspicious orientation according to the ancient principles of *feng shui* or geomancy[1]. The store was located close to the entrance to town, east of the Union Hotel. By the mid-1860s, there were other Chinese dwellings between the hotel and the Chew Kee Store. Today a tennis court and public park occupy the space where once the hotel (later replaced by a large barn) and the other structures stood.

DOCTOR YEE FUNG CHEUNG, HERBALIST

Family stories relate that Yee Fung Cheung set out for Gold Mountain around 1850, two years before the major influx of Chinese miners to California. He was about twenty-five years old, leaving behind a wife and four children—two sons and two daughters. He hailed from Sing Tong village in Toishan (formerly Sunning) County in the Guangdong Province.

Arriving by ship in San Francisco, Yee Fung Cheung first went to Sacramento and then made his way to Fiddletown, known for its rich placer discoveries. Before reverting to his profession, it is said that he tried his luck mining creeks and ravines for gold. He was trained in China in the ancient science of herbal medicine, and this proved to be a much

---

1 The word literally means "wind-water," connected with the Taoist philosophical concept of harmony with nature and the earth's flow of energy. Chinese immigrants applied its principles to orient buildings and graves to harmonize with the surrounding environment.

Figure 9. Chew Kee Store. *Ron Scofield*

more lucrative prospect in frontier California than the difficult work of extracting gold from gravel. Consequently, between the mid-1850s and 1860, Dr. Yee Fung Cheung established his herbal practice on Fiddletown's main street in the rammed earth building. His skills were valuable not only to Chinese inhabitants of Fiddletown, but perhaps also to nearby Americans and Europeans, who may have ventured into his shop after learning about the efficacy of his cures. He prescribed remedies for both men and women, including prostitutes who worked in Fiddletown. Some of the ailments that he treated were convulsions, menstrual disorders, rheumatoid arthritis, fever, gastrointestinal problems, lung disorders and pain. People with infections from wounds, insect bites, headaches, bronchitis, digestive problems, anxiety or depression and other maladies would visit the herb doctor. Among the remedies, ginger was used for nausea and digestion; ginkgo biloba for asthma, bronchitis and kidney disorders; medicinal balm for headaches, dizziness and insect bites; lychee for treating diarrhea and quenching thirst. Dr. Yee Fung Cheung may have saved many lives in this pioneer environment, where infection could be deadly.

CHINESE MEDICINE

Chinese herbal medicine, originating about five thousand years ago, was systematized and formalized in written texts at a time when western medicine was still in a rudimentary stage. It rested on philosophical principles of harmony achieved through balance between opposing yet complementary forces of nature, *yin* and *yang*: female/male, dark/bright, moon/sun, cold/hot, wet/ dry, etc. Disease was considered an imbalance in yin and yang; food and good health were interrelated. Treatment of illness emphasized restoring balance in the body through diet and herbal prescriptions, food being the first course of treatment. Herbal remedies were prescribed for specific maladies and they also addressed promoting vital energy (qi) and replenishing organs and body fluids, principles intrinsic to Chinese medicine.

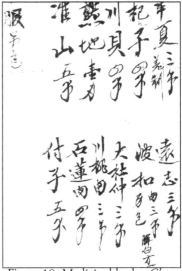

Figure 10. Medicinal herbs. *Chew Kee Store*

Both food and herbs from China were imported to California in a vigorous trade that commenced early on to meet the needs of Chinese living in a strange new world. Chinese immigrants, even those mining in camps along rivers and streams, were able to maintain their traditional diet—a healthy diet that included the staple of rice along with such foods as dried fish, preserved vegetables such as salted cabbage, fermented bean curd, and other ingredients that made for a balanced diet. The Chinese boiled water for drinking and making tea, which prevented illnesses such as dysentery, cholera and diarrhea. Still, the Chinese working and living in the area were subject to injury, maladies and disease.

Chinese doctors made (and still make) their diagnosis based on four steps: 1) Observing (*wang*) the appearance of the patient, such as face color, eyes and tongue in particular; 2) Listening (*wen*) to what the patient reports about his or her condition; 3) Asking (*wen*) the patient questions; 4. Touching (*che*) the patient's wrist to get the pulse. Pulse points along the arteries on both wrists correspond to various organs of the body.

Figure 11. Yee Fung Cheung's herb drawers. *D. Zorbas*

THE HERBAL PHARMACY

The herb store functioned as a pharmacy or apothecary shop. Yee Fung Cheung had on hand about 150 herbs, the essential number for practicing herbal medicine. Ingredients included asparagus root, bitter apricot kernel, lily bulb, tangerine peel, magnolia bark, licorice root, sweet basil, and other plant and animal components (such as horn or earthworm) unfamiliar to westerners. They were carefully arranged in twenty-five drawers, each divided into four or six sections and labeled with Chinese characters to identify their contents. Different parts of a plant—flower, leaf, bark, stalk, seed, rind and root—were chosen to treat various medical conditions and diseases. Herbs were collected, winnowed and dried in baskets found throughout the store. Some ingredients were ground into a paste with a mortar and pestle for external use. The mortar and pestle are still in the store.

Yee Fung Cheung prepared prescription packets for his patients, combining herbs and seeds and other components as needed. It was essential that the doctor understood the properties of the various ingredients by prescribing the correct dosage to avoid side effects and possible toxins. Most of the ingredients were imported from China. Each prescription was customized to treat the specific ailment of the patient, who would take the herbal concoction wrapped in a small paper packet, to be boiled into tea or broth best done in earthenware vessels. The brew could be very bitter.

Yee Fung Cheung first appears in public records in 1863-4 under the name Yee Fung when he was taxed by the federal government (the IRS was created during the Civil War) for owning thirteen to sixteen hogs. Pigs were roasted by Chinese for special occasions, and also sold for meat to people of all nationalities. A few years later in 1866, he was taxed for retail liquor, most likely Chinese wine sold at the herb shop.

Figure 12. Chew Kee Store altar. *Daniel D'Agostini*

45

SETTING UP SHOP: CULTURAL TRANSPLANTATION

Dr. Yee Fung Cheung used the rammed earth Chinese building as his place of work and home. The thick walls kept the store cool during the hot California summers. So did oblong and round holes in the wooden floor in the back hall which allowed cool air from under the building to flow upwards. Iron shutters and iron doors protected the store from the fires that ravaged Sierra Nevada mining towns. The front iron door was forged by Fiddletown blacksmith Christopher Schallhorn, whose massive blacksmith and wagon stop still dominates Fiddletown's Main Street.

The herb doctor furnished the commercial part of his enterprise in a manner typical of Chinese herb stores, with many drawers for herbs, display cases, a long service counter, and high shelves for storage. The front room of the building was used for transacting business, separated from the living area in back by double doors with a window to view customers entering the store. Over those doors a banner with four large characters in red still offers wishes for *a harmonious union between the Chinese and barbarians* (i.e. Westerners or foreigners). An inscription by the double doors, "*spirit essence of dragon and horse,*" conveys wishes for longevity. Chinese culture is infused with symbolism. Red is a propitious color; the dragon symbolizes protection and good fortune; longevity is most

Figure 13. Commercial front of the store. *D. Zorbas*

prized among human conditions. On each Chinese New Year, Yee Fung Cheung and later occupants hung four red Chinese characters by the sides of the double doors to express wishes for happiness, fortune, prosperity and longevity. Red and gold strips of paper were appended across all doorways,

Figure 14. Medicine and prescription packets.
Laura Faye Mah

perforated with small holes to allow good spirits to come through, preventing bad spirits from entering. These banners and ornaments remain in the Chew Kee Store.

For spiritual guidance, the herb doctor's shop contained an altar in the front room where he could give offerings to ancestors and appeal to gods for good luck, prosperity and intervention with misfortune. There were two sections to the altar. The lower part was dedicated to the deity of the earth with a written supplication to protect the wealth of the store, invoking both Chinese and Western gods. In the upper altar, the herb doctor and his successors gave offerings such as food, fruit and flowers to ancestors and burned incense to communicate with the spirit world and to fend off evil. Three deities, painted in the background of the altar, represented fortune (*fu*), prosperity (*lu*), and longevity (*shau*).

Yee Fung Cheung's private living quarters were behind the double doors, set off from the commercial part of the store. The herb doctor must have been small in stature, because the viewing window into the front area is very low. The back rooms consisted of his bedroom with a bed made of planks and a small office to the left of a short hall. In the office, he could prepare bills using an abacus, write prescriptions for customers, and compose letters to send to his family in China. The office had another board bed and an upper loft area for storage that could also accommodate itinerant Chinese miners who needed a place to sleep. The interior walls, wood floors and furniture were hand-hewn, crudely put together with whatever boards could be found.

To Chinese customers, the commercial storefront was familiar and reassuring, evoking similar stores back home in China. To American and

European customers, the Chinese herb shop introduced them to a very different culture, well beyond their experience. Motivated by illness, they needed to overcome cultural barriers, step down into the cool, dark interior and make the leap into the strange, dark quarters where the skilled herb doctor could potentially offer a cure.

EXPANSION OF THE YEE ENTERPRISE

Being an enterprising sort, Dr. Yee Fung Cheung had the business instinct to go where his skills were needed. He expanded his business to Sacramento, known to the Chinese as *Yee Fow* or "Second City" (the first city was San Francisco). There he gave medical treatment to Chinese workers who came from Guangdong Province to construct the western portion of the transcontinental railway, work that was risky and hazardous, often resulting in injury and death.

Yee Fung Cheung's next destination for expanding his herb business was Virginia City, Nevada, which had attracted Chinese during the big silver strike known as the Comstock Lode and during railroad construction in Nevada. In 1869, his younger son, Yee Lok Sam, came from China to join him. Together with another partner, they established their medical practice in Virginia City in October 1869, the same year that the transcontinental railroad was completed.[2]

Two years later, Yee Fung Cheung was back in Fiddletown purchasing property at the time when the town site plan was officially created. He was granted certificates in 1871 showing ownership of two properties on Main Street. Under the name Yee Fung & Co. he acquired the gambling house opposite the herb store in the heart of Chinatown, and as Yee Fung he acquired another parcel, two lots to the east of the store on the north side of Main Street. Although he never formally obtained the deeds to these properties, they became known in records as the "Yee Fung properties." In 1878 he was assessed taxes for three different parcels in other parts of town, two on the street behind Dry Creek (Jibboom, known as Back Street). These properties had previously belonged to H.A. Kutchenthal, a longtime Fiddletown resident. Yee Fung Cheung must have purchased them and used them as rentals. Under the name E. Fung, the herb doctor is listed on indexes to Fiddletown property records from 1881 through 1889. No detailed records of the properties are extant.

---

2 Choy, Philip P. *Canton Footprints: Sacramento's Chinese Legacy*. (Sacramento, Chinese American Council of Sacramento, 2007), pg. 22.

With three herb stores to maintain, Dr. Yee Fung Cheung must have relied on assistants or relatives to manage his Fiddletown property as he moved from location to location. A Chinese language record found in the Chew Kee Store[3] includes information about Yee Yun who along with his elder brother ran a different Yee Fung business than the herb store. His wife, Yee Lee Sai Ngun, originally from Sze Yup, came to Fiddletown from Sacramento in 1886. Two years later, their sons arrived in Fiddletown: Yee King Cheung, age eight, and Yee Duk, age two. Mrs. Yee died in 1889, and her husband continued to run the Yee Fung business for a year afterwards. He then departed for Sacramento with his sons. It is possible that this Yee family was related to Yee Fung Cheung or originated from the same clan.

Legend goes that Dr. Yee was able to cure patients with a "dose of his smile." Family stories relate that his most renowned cure involved treating Mrs. Leland Stanford, who was gravely ill from a severe pulmonary condition. Apparently all other resources had been exhausted before Dr. Yee was summoned. Applying his knowledge of herbal qualities, he was able to cure Mrs. Stanford by brewing a tea using Ma Huang, a natural source of ephedrine, effective in treating bronchitis. This was ironical because when Leland Stanford was California Governor (1862-1863), he was strongly anti-Chinese, urging taxation to stem Chinese immigration. Only in 1865, as one of the Big Four financiers of the Central Pacific Railroad, did he finally recognize the abilities of Chinese workers—acknowledging their patience, industriousness and efficiency, while shrewdly observing that they were willing to work for lower wages. He must have been taken aback when Chinese railroad workers went on strike for higher wages a few years later.

Yee Fung Cheung's second and youngest son, Yee Lok Sam was also an herbalist who later became known as T. Wah Hing (the "T" being a misunderstanding by Americans of Yee). Knowledge of herbal medicine was often transferred within a Chinese family from generation to generation.

There are two versions of the how the name *Wah Hing* was appended to the Yee name. In one, the herb doctor was playing mah jong at a grocery store named Wah Hing when he was urged by the Stanford family cook to come to the rescue of Mrs. Stanford. Somehow the store name was confused with his own. Dr. Herbert K. Yee, great-grandson of the original herb doctor, explained in a 1978 interview:

3　Translated from the Fiddletown *Cemetery Record Book* by Dr. Sonia Ng.

They marveled at this Chinese doctor who did such a miraculous feat. No one knew what his name was, but they mentioned that they picked him up at the Wah Hing Store. So from then on he was known as—they misspelled his name, they called him T. instead of Yee—T. Wah Hing, and he was so famous that consequently that name went on and his son took it.[4]

The other explanation is that *Wah Hing* was another first name. As mentioned earlier, in China a person can have different names depending on age and position. The historian Philip Choy obtained an 1886 document from China that used the name Wah Hing in reference to Dr. Yee Fung Cheung's practice in Virginia City. As described in the book *Canton Footprints*[5], that document, coming from Hong Kong, provided proof that Wah Hing had the education and qualifications to be an herb doctor, refuting challenges from envious white doctors who had questioned his credentials. He also used the name Wah Hing professionally when he returned to Sacramento in 1901 to set up his medical office. The herb store in Fiddletown was in the past, but not forgotten.

Dr. Yee Fung Cheung spent his final California years practicing herbal medicine in Sacramento, before departing for his village in China where he died in 1907. His son Yee Lok Sam (also known as T. Wah Hing) made his life in California, bringing his family to join him. Along with his father, he established an office in 1901 as a physician and surgeon, first at 707 J Street, then at 725 J Street in Sacramento, where he continued to practice herbal medicine for the next thirty years. Known for his skill as an herbalist, he treated both Chinese and white patients.

4 Wey, Nancy. "Oral History Interview with Dr. Herbert Yee, Great-Grandson of Dr. Fan-Chung Yee." June 4, 1978. Transcript of tape recording. *Nancy Wey Papers*, Ethnic Studies Library, University of California, Berkeley.
5 Choy, pg. 22.

PROPERTY OWNERSHIP AND TOWN PLANS

Although parcels in the different towns of Amador County were bought, sold, and recorded in previous decades, town plans were formalized in 1870-71. Judges issued certificates and awarded deeds to Chinese residents as well as other property owners. Maps of the various towns defined where the Chinatowns were.

FIDDLETOWN

In the town plan formalized in 1871, Fiddletown's Chinatown is delineated by a seasonal creek or gulch originating in hills to the south. Former Deputy Sheriff W.T. Gist, who had by then moved to Sacramento, purchased parcels on both sides of this creek south of Main Street. The other American landowner in Chinatown, Mrs. Goff, owned property next to Gist as well as several lots across the street. Her parcels at the west end of town were bordered by Chinese landowners. There is a good possibility that the Chinese section extended even further west, beyond the town boundaries. Contemporary residents have found traces of Chinese gardens past Main Street in the hills to the northwest. One local story tells of Chinese workers rising at three o'clock in the morning to walk from Fiddletown where they raised vegetables, to Volcano ten miles away, carrying their produce in baskets supported by a long horizontal pole braced over their shoulders. Many Chinese immigrants, especially from the county of Toishan, had experience as farmers.

As shown on the town site map, Foo Kee, Yee Fung, and Wo Sing owned parcels along west Main Street. Both Foo Kee and Wo Sing were merchants. Yee Fung is most likely the herb doctor, Yee Fung Cheung, whose shop operated as a pharmacy in the Chew Kee Store. All of these men obtained business licenses, along with another merchant, Lee Kee.

The Fiddletown town plan shows a long 4.35 acre parcel designated as "Chinese." This was owned by the merchant Foo Kee, who will be discussed in another chapter. The parcel encompasses a steep hill, which would place any Chinese houses at the crest and not on the slopes. The number of structures and their occupants is not known, although in general Chinese living quarters were crowded, some with twelve to fourteen people in a single household.

Figure 15. Fiddletown seasonal creek. *D. Zorbas*

The Chew Kee Store lot does not appear on the town site map. Its location (block 4, lot 10), on the north side of Main Street, is part of larger parcel that was sold in 1870 to E.C. Simpson, a 47 year-old miner. Mention is made in the deed of the Union Hotel and its barn, but nothing was noted about the rammed-earth store. From this lack of reference, it is evident that the herb store was allowed to squat on this property—in addition to other structures occupied by Chinese.

OTHER TOWNS

In Drytown China Street ran south and west of Main Street, crossing Dry Creek. The merchant On Hop and a man called Ah Ling owned parcels along that street in two areas of town—one by the road to Ione, the other behind Main Street, next to parcels owned by whites. Presumably, the rest of the town's Chinese were renters. The Chinese population, although consisting mostly of miners, also had people involved in diverse occupations: barber, baker, laborer, saloon keeper, physician, cook, grocer, merchant, butcher, blacksmith assistant—the same array of professions necessary to sustain mining communities.

In Jackson more deeds were taken out by Chinese than in other communities, formalizing purchases of small lots on the west side of north Main Street. Some of them had been bought in the 1860s. Several people clustered together in contiguous properties: Him Lung, Cum Sing,

Ah Coon, Ah Sam, Ti Wah, and Ah Hee. Merchants and partners Ah Ping (Ah Paeng) and Chung Sun (Chung Sung) owned two parcels across the street. These properties were interspersed with those owned by whites. Although situated right next to the town's busy commercial center, the location of Jackson's Chinatown, which bridged both sides of the north fork of Jackson Creek, later proved to be unfortunate.

In Lancha Plana, a one-and-one-third acre plot next to Chinatown was devoted to Chinese gardens. Vegetables were probably grown and sold to both the Chinese and white communities in surrounding areas. See Foy owned the three parcels that encompassed the gardens and Chinatown, together consisting of more than three acres. This ownership may have been shared collectively among the Chinese community as represented by See Foy. Lancha Plana Chinatown was located off an alley leading to the Mokelumne River where there was abundant water for maintaining the gardens.

Ione's Chinatown was located east of the center of town off Main Street on the crest of a hill overlooking the creek. It occupied 5.22 acres as shown on the town site map, but there are no listings of Chinese property owners. Most likely, the Chinese squatted on unclaimed land. In 1883, merchants Hop Wah Chung, Ky Kee, Queng On Lang, and the Chang Hang Co. formally purchased the property from the Ione Coal & Iron Company.

TRANSACTIONS BETWEEN CHINESE OWNERS

Among themselves, the Chinese also bought and sold property, adhering to standard business practices. An interesting contract found in the Chew Kee Store[1] formalized the sale of a house in Fiddletown having two upstairs rooms. Initially purchased by a Chinese person from a white American, the Chinese owner was later in need of money to return to Guangdong Province. So he put the property up for sale again. A couple from Punyu County in Guangdong, Tse Kim and Sai Ngun, bought the house for sixty dollars. The seller assured the couple that they could stay in the house trouble-free. On April 15, 1881, the sales agreement was confirmed in a written contract "since verbal agreement has no basis," as stated in the document. The receipt for the payment was signed by Sui Sum, a woman who also contributed to charities in Fiddletown.

---

1 Translated by Kai Lui, San Francisco, 2006 and reviewed by Dr. Sonia Ng.

ENTREPRENEURS AND MERCHANTS

For two thousand years the most highly regarded occupation in China was to be a scholar and serve in the imperial civil service, open to any young man who passed stringent written examinations. Merchants were at the bottom of the social ladder. But California offered tremendous opportunities to merchants, who often prospered in this new environment and later received preferential legal status. They also became leaders in Chinese communities.

ROLE OF CHINESE STORES

With the influx of Chinese to the U.S., an import-export trade developed that benefited merchants in the new world and enterprises back in Hong Kong. By the mid-1850s, establishments in Hong Kong, called Gold Mountain firms, were able to fulfill the demand for goods and services needed by Chinese living in California. Products were shipped from Hong Kong to San Francisco and from there to distribution points in Sacramento, Stockton and Marysville, all along major rivers. Chinese Camp in Tuolumne County to the south was also a major conduit for supplying Chinese labor and products. Orders for foodstuff, newspapers, magazines, utensils, clothing and other specialized items were filled and delivered to Chinese in the mining camps and towns through a series of relationships, often via relatives or people from the same district or village.

Merchandise stores provided other important services to their Chinese communities, especially critical because of the written language differences. Since Chinese writing was inscrutable to Americans, letters from China were conveyed to and from stores in care of their merchants (store names written in English). Their trajectory could include going from the village to Guangzhou (Canton City), then to Hong Kong, arriving in San Francisco and sent from there to a store in Stockton, and finally to Fiddletown or another destination. Letters would be held until they could be picked up in the local community where the addressee was staying. Letters to China (often written by a literate merchant or herb doctor) were kept at the store, waiting for relatives or contacts heading for San Francisco. They would then be transported by the designated carrier on to Hong Kong and from there distributed to the home village.

Figure 16. Sing Kee and wife. *Amador County Archives*

Earnings from gold mining or other labor often were held in Chinese stores, gold dust converted into coin, and from there conveyed to family in China through trusted friends and relatives. Some stores acted as credit unions, retaining and lending savings from the community as will be seen in Fiddletown in conjunction with the Chinese cemetery.

The importing of Chinese goods allowed Chinese immigrants to continue their way of life in which food and health were so intertwined. Rice and tea were basic to the diet; Chinese dried and preserved seafood, vegetables, condiments and fruits were vital to health and well-being. Chopsticks, patterned rice bowls and dishware, small cups, wok cookware and teapots were part of Chinese households in the U.S. and must have been curious items to Americans, unacquainted with the customs and practices of people from Asia.

Many of these items, especially fragments of porcelain bowls, plates, and cups, have been excavated in our times by archeologists. Decorative tableware in patterns common to the nineteenth century and early twentieth century China have been found in Fiddletown and Drytown, as well as brown stoneware vessels, still present in the Chew Kee Store.

AMADOR COUNTY MERCHANTS

Many Chinese merchants did business in Amador County towns for decades. They provided continuity and merchandise to the Chinese communities. It should be noted that prices tended to be lower in Chinese stores, and therefore Americans were among the customers. Also the Chinese entrepreneurial spirit was very much in synch with American values, which prizes business and monetary success above all.

Business license records tracking Drytown in the 1860s reveal an active commercial section. In July 1863, six Chinese merchants obtained business licenses. In the 1867 Chinatown fire, the main losers were merchants: Ky On [Kie Owen], Hi Co., Chung Lee & Co. and Ah Young & Co. Although Kie Owen and Ah Young were among those who lost their stores in the fire, the following year both were back in business along with Hing Kee, On Hop, On Key, and Tong Chung.

Prominent Chinese merchants were also evident in other communities: Ti Wah and Chung Sung in Jackson, Sing Kee and his wife in Volcano, Sun Ming Gee (or Ah Ming) in Plymouth. Ione merchants Hop Wah Chung, Ky (Kie) Kee were prominent; Ling Sing Tong Co. also operated in Ione City.

When the Jackson merchant Tung Paeng (also referred to in records as Ah Ping) died on August 15, 1872, his widow Sun Hee handled the estate. Tung Paeng was in partnership with Tung Quen and died while in San Francisco buying merchandise for their business, the Chung Soon Company. It appears that Amador County merchants periodically went to San Francisco for business, a trip that must have taken at least a day by stagecoach.[1]

The store in Jackson had a huge inventory, detailed in the probate record: foodstuff that included 20 pounds of dried shrimp, 100 pounds of China sugar, 27 sacks of rice, 50 pounds of peanuts, and 30 pounds of green ginger. Other stock consisted of 50 bunches of firecrackers, 30 pounds of washing soap, 60 gallons of brandy and paper for tobacco and funerals, as well as clothing, mining equipment, cooking and eating vessels and utensils. The list of merchandise demonstrates that food, clothing, implements for eating and cooking, and funeral paraphernalia were readily available to Chinese immigrants and residents. Many items were sold on credit, a practice common among Chinese merchants.

---

1 San Francisco is 120 miles from Fiddletown, a three hour trip by automobile.

Fiddletown had the most consistency of merchants who settled in town. The merchants Foo Kee, Lee Kee, and Wo Sing started operating stores in the 1860s and continued in business throughout most of the nineteenth century. The presence of these and other merchants for decades in Amador County communities shows that they had established a settled life in California where there was more opportunity to prosper than in Guangdong.

FOO KEE, FIDDLETOWN MERCHANT AND LEADER

Among Fiddletown's merchants in the 1870s to mid-1880s, Foo Kee was the wealthiest and a leader in the Chinese community. He was among the first four Chinese merchants to obtain business licenses in Fiddletown. He owned more property than any other Chinese person. He was also donor and custodian of funds to build and maintain Fiddletown's Chinese cemetery.

Significantly, his merchandise store is still standing on the south side of Fiddletown's Main Street, a solid and substantial two-story brick building, known as the Chinese General Store. Constructed in the late 1850s or early 1860s, most likely by Americans, this structure could not easily be destroyed by the fires so prevalent in mining towns. It has therefore has survived into the twenty-first century.

Little is known about the merchant Foo Kee, even his true surname. In Chinese, *Foo* means rich and full of fortune; *Kee* means store. There was a Foo Kee in Jackson between 1863 and 1866 who was a peddler and who owned as many as forty hogs at one time. In 1866, he was taxed

Figure 17. Fiddletown Chinese General Store. *Ron Scofield*

for selling retail liquor. This man may have acquired enough wealth to move to Fiddletown, purchase property and establish a store. When the lots on Fiddletown town site were surveyed and delineated in 1871, Foo Kee obtained certificates awarded by the judge for three properties. He was resourceful enough to subsequently obtain the proper licenses and deeds from the county seat of Jackson. The 1870 Census identified him as a forty-seven-year-old merchant who employed three Chinese store clerks. In addition, a Chinese miner and a thirty-two year old woman named Sing Choy resided with Foo Kee. Whether Sing Choy was a wife or concubine is unknown. She was described as "keeping house," a term that also applied to Caucasian housewives.

Chinese and other merchandise stores in the gold regions carried all sorts of provisions tailored to their communities. Foo Kee no doubt purchased goods from Hong Kong companies through distributors and stores in San Francisco and Sacramento, and in some cases locally in Amador County. Visitors to the Foo Kee General Store could obtain a variety of merchandise, including:

- preserved food such as salted cabbage, dried fish, salted ginger, dried mushrooms, peanuts, canned oysters and other fish
- bulk staples such as rice, tea, flour, sugar, vinegar and barley
- fresh vegetables, fruits, pork, chicken and fish
- cooking and eating implements such as chopsticks, woks, pans, cleavers, rice bowls, large cooking bowls and willow baskets
- cigarettes, cigars, tobacco, Chinese wine, brandy, opium, opium pipes and lamps
- Chinese and American-style clothing, including shoes and boots
- Chinese writing paper, ink and brushes, white funeral paper, candles, abacuses, firecrackers, dominos, dice, playing cards and blank account books and ledgers

As with other merchandise stores owned by Europeans and Americans, the Foo Kee General Store would have also sold oil lamps, heating oil, shovels, picks, scales for weighing gold, brooms, soap, mirrors, clocks and a variety of other objects needed for daily living and mining.

Foo Kee's other properties were located on the south side of Main Street behind structures, including his own store. The largest was a parcel of over four acres, marked "Chinese" on the 1871 town site map of Fiddletown. Foo Kee may have rented houses to Chinese tenants on this parcel and on another smaller lot. Only a one-room house remains, constructed of adobe blocks with eighteen-inch-thick walls. It rests on flat land carved from the hillside, with a high ceiling and a loft reachable only via the supporting hill. Constructed by Chinese workers, the use of the building is unknown and it is now privately owned. A bill of sale for lumber worth $190 was found on the site, made out to QKee & Company [writing difficult to decipher].

A smaller lot owned by Foo Kee was adjacent to the seasonal creek that delineated Chinatown. It consists of a strip of land on one side of the creek that gently slopes with some level areas. Chinese residents could make good use of the proximity to water. On the opposite side of the creek a year-round spring provided ample water on land owned by Gist but probably rented to Chinese. The creek flowed during the winter and spring, and flat areas on both sides were ideal sites for growing fresh vegetables, an essential part of the Chinese diet. Was this parcel used as community property? A Chinese "pig oven" for roasting pork and the remains of a well still stand on that lot, an indication that the area was a gathering site for Fiddletown's Chinese community where festive

Figure 18. Chinese adobe building. *D.Zorbas*

60

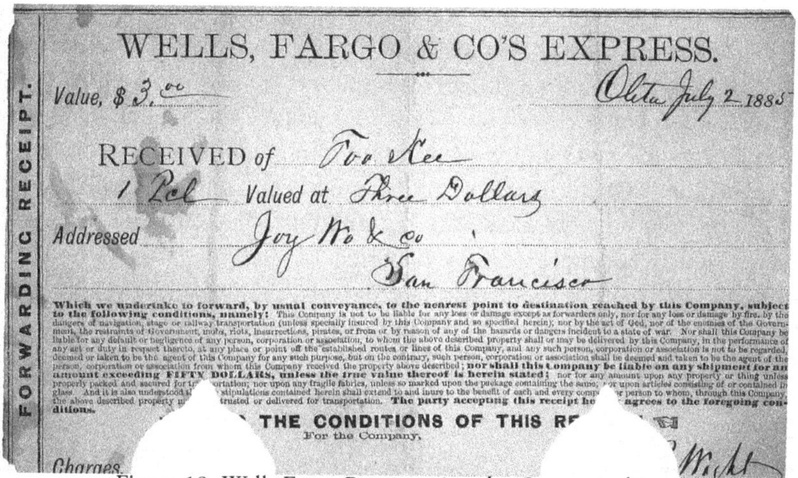
FORWARDING RECEIPT.

WELLS, FARGO & CO'S EXPRESS.

Value, $ 3.00 Oleta July 2 1885

RECEIVED of Foo Kee

1 Pcl Valued at Three Dollars

Addressed Joy Wo & Co

San Francisco

Which we undertake to forward, by usual conveyance, to the nearest point to destination reached by this Company, subject to the following conditions, namely: This Company is not to be liable for any loss or damage except as forwarders only, nor for any loss or damage by fire, by the dangers of navigation, stage or railway transportation (unless specially insured by this Company and so specified herein); nor by the act of God, nor of the enemies of the Government, the restraints of Government, mobs, riots, insurrections, pirates, or from or by reason of any of the hazards or dangers incident to a state of war. Nor shall this Company be liable for any default or negligence of any person, corporation or association, to whom the above described property shall or may be delivered by this Company, in the performance of any act or duty in respect thereto, at any place or point off the established routes or lines of this Company, and any such person, corporation or association is not to be regarded, deemed or taken to be the agent of this Company for any such purpose, but on the contrary, such person, corporation or association shall be deemed and taken to be the agent of the person, corporation or association from whom this Company received the property above described; **nor shall this Company be liable on any shipment for an amount exceeding FIFTY DOLLARS, unless the true value thereof is herein stated;** nor for any amount upon any property or thing unless properly packed and secured for tr[illegible]ortation; nor upon any fragile fabrics, unless so marked upon the package containing the same; [illegible]or upon articles consisting of or contained in glass. And it is also understood t[illegible] stipulations contained herein shall extend to and inure to the benefit of each and every comp[illegible] or person to whom, through this Company, the above described property m[illegible] trusted or delivered for transportation. **The party accepting this receipt he[illegible] agrees to the foregoing conditions.**

[illegible] THE CONDITIONS OF THIS RE[illegible]

For the Company,

Charges [illegible] Wickt

Figure 19. Wells Fargo Receipt. *Amador County Archives*

occasions such as the Chinese New Year could be celebrated. How the aromas of sizzling roast pork must have wafted through the town!

Yet this smaller lot was sold for a pittance by Foo Kee in 1873 to W.T. Gist with the proviso that a barn and stable on the southeast corner along with access to Main Street be reserved for another longtime Chinese merchant Wo Sing, who owned a store opposite the Chew Kee Store. Gist was the former constable who had bought up several properties in the Chinese section of town in the 1860s and was currently living in Sacramento. By purchasing Foo Kee's parcel, Gist now owned front and back property bordering the creek, an area critical for supplying water throughout the year.

Foo Kee was well off compared to other Chinese residents. In the 1870 Census, his real estate was valued at $500 and his personal estate at $1,500. This was substantially more than any other Chinese merchant, although less than American merchants. For example the real estate of James Head, who owned the town's general store, was valued at $3000 and his personal estate valued at $8,000.

The whereabouts of Foo Kee's living quarters is not known. He may have lived in his store, as did many Chinese merchants. An undated work order referred to the amount of wood required to build Foo Kee's kitchen—1,289 separate pieces consisting of ten types of logs and boards. Foo Kee was willing to pay for as many as fifteen hundred pieces. In 1878-79, he was assessed for a house and lot in Fiddletown, as well as a mining claim in Upper Rancheria, known as the Rice Claim. His personal property was then valued at $1,140.

After 1886 Foo Kee's name disappears from extant records. He was then in his sixties and most likely returned to his village in China to live out his life in comfort with the wealth earned on Gold Mountain. He may have had a wife and children waiting for him in China.

His store and the two parcels occupied by Chinese were relegated to the merchant Chew Kee, who became custodian of many properties abandoned by Chinese as they departed Fiddletown. After Chew Kee gained possession of them, all three parcels, including the one that had been sold to Gist, were referred to in public records as the "Foo Kee property."

LABORERS AND THE ANTI-CHINESE MOVEMENT

Men from China, many from the county of Toishan, had been recruited to come to the U.S. between 1864 and 1869 to provide labor for building the Central Pacific Railroad across the formidable Sierra Nevada mountain range. The 1868 Burlingame Treaty with China permitted Chinese to immigrate to the U.S., granting China a most favored nation status and giving its citizens reciprocal privileges as foreign nationals. As many as twelve thousand Chinese workers were employed at the peak of construction, enduring danger and deprivation as they blasted tunnels through the mountains and hacked lines for rails above precipitous cliffs. Thanks to their skill, fortitude and perseverance, the western link of the transcontinental railroad was completed one year ahead of schedule. In October 1869, eastern and western legs of the railroad were joined at Promontory Point in Utah, thereby transforming transportation in the United States. Chinese workers were not given credit for this huge accomplishment.

Hard times lay ahead in the 1870s as white labor became organized. Unemployment following the depression of 1873 led to virulent anti-Chinese actions in which the Chinese were blamed for taking jobs from whites and working for lower wages. Legal barriers and mob agitation started in San Francisco and Sacramento and reverberated into the mining areas.

In 1870 the U.S. Census counted 1,627 Chinese living in Amador County, or 16 percent of the county's population, and probably more because of undercounting. Townships with the largest proportion of Chinese residents were Fiddletown (28 percent), Drytown (21 percent), Ione (24 percent), and Jackson (17 percent). The towns had active Chinese communities, with an array of merchandise and grocery stores, barber shops, boarding houses, eating places, gambling and opium establishments, houses of prostitution, laundries, temples, associations, herb shops and gardens.

Chinese residents were employed throughout the county as hotel and restaurant cooks, bakers, butchers, household servants, farm workers and mine workers. As laborers, they worked for white employers by building roads, chopping wood, and digging ditches and canals to divert and bring water to mining areas. Chinese were paid lower wages and toiled long hours on these projects that helped build the infrastructure of the county.[1]

MINING SUCCESS AND BARRIERS

Immigrant Chinese continued to extract gold from placer mining in Amador County long after industrial quartz mines became the main producers of gold ore. The local newspaper in 1870 reported some success—gold uncovered by Chinese in creek ground that had been worked over at least a dozen times; a party of Chinese who extracted $10,000 to $12,000 from a claim purchased near Jackson for $400. The *Weekly Ledger* writer observed, "Patient toil will meet its return." In July 1878 the newspaper reported, "Nearly all the gold sold to Jackson merchants is by Chinamen. Chinamen monopolize the placer mining in the neighborhood. They manage to get considerable gold, and it is thought they make on average $2 per day per man."

Overall, mining had shifted from being an independent endeavor to a heavily capitalized enterprise in which miners and other workers were the hired hands. Many mines were owned by absentee investors in San Francisco. Chinese laborers were willing to do whatever work was available, but immigrants of other ethnicities—Italian, Austrian, Cornish, Irish, Serbian—competed for jobs in the deep quartz rock mines. When labor in Amador County became organized, the miner's union attempted to bar Chinese from working in the gold mines.

THE AMADOR WAR

The Amador County Laborer's Association, later known as the Miners' League was formed in July 1870 "for the protection of white labor, to maintain its dignity, and secure fair compensation therefore [sic], to discourage competition of inferior races."[2] Less than a year later on June 1, 1871, the Miners' League, with about five hundred members, called for a strike if demands were not met. Their purpose was primarily to be paid slightly higher wages, $3 for a ten-hour day for first hands (engineers, blasters) and $2.50 second hands (all other workers including

---

1 There is no documentary evidence that Chinese workers provided labor to build the dry rock walls prevalent in parts of the county farmed by Italian immigrants. However, it is possible that Italian farmers may have hired Chinese as well as other ethnicities to do the heavy work of excavating and moving rocks.

2 *Sacramento Daily Union*, June 23, 1871.

Figure 20. Oneida gold mine. *Amador County Archives*

surface men and mill workers who had been paid $2.25). But also at issue was preventing employment of Chinese labor in the mines.

Mine owners refused to capitulate to the workers, and the Miners' League ordered a work stoppage. The strike continued for several weeks, shutting down and damaging the large mines. Fearing both loss of profit and the potential of violence from the strikers (exaggerated by the press), mine owners prevailed upon the California State Governor to send four hundred troops from the National Guard, who arrived in Sutter Creek on June 26. The conflict was called "The Amador War," but actually the mines began working again and negotiations with the League were peaceful. On July 5, the miners agreed to a compromise proposed by the mine owners in which all men working underground would be paid $2.50 and $3 per day; those on the surface would continue to be paid "to their worth," not a big gain. Furthermore, "the employment of Chinese will be discouraged…" The final settlement was stalled when the Superintendent of the Oneida Mine, James Morgan, withdrew his approval stating that he wanted to employ Chinese in his stamp mill.[3]

---

3 Heaney, Thomas, "By the Sword Still Sheathed: The Miners, the Militia, and the Amador War of 1871" (paper for History 191, Sacramento State, Fall 1989). Located in the Amador County Archives, this paper gives a detailed account of the Amador War.

On July 13, the Oneida Mine Superintendent conceded and agreed not to employ Chinese. The President of the Miners' League response was printed in the *Daily Alta California*, July 15, 1871:

> While the miners do not claim the right to prevent Morgan, or any other man, from employing Chinese labor, they do claim the right to uphold and maintain the dignity of white labor by refusing to work for those who employ Chinamen, and by calling upon their white brethren to do likewise.

Payroll records from the Oneida Mine[4] show that despite threats from white miners, the company continued to hire Chinese labor for years, primarily in the stamp mill where rocks were crushed. In the fall of 1871, nine Chinese were hired as mill hands and paid either $1.50 or $1.75 a day. For a brief period between 1872 and 1874, two to three Chinese men were permitted to work in the mine as car men, receiving a higher compensation of $2 per day. They were subsequently replaced in that position by whites. Chinese employees remained working as surface workers in the stamp mill for $1.75 per day. These men performed hard unskilled labor such as breaking rocks, piling wood and shoveling, and thus were limited to jobs that paid lower wages. Skilled Caucasian workers in the mine earned between $2.50 and $3.50 per day; blacksmiths and machinists made as much as $4 daily.

Chinese laborers were employed in other types of industrial mines in the county, again for lower wages than other employees. In the late 1870s, over one hundred Chinese workers extracted coal from the Carbondale Coal Mine in Ione for a pittance—three and one-half cents per day; $10 per month. At the Newton Copper Mine in the same area, half the workers were Chinese. The newspaper reported, "It is possible that a number of mines would be unable to work in the absence of this cheap labor. Nevertheless, these moon-eyed helpers are a drag upon any community..."

EXTENDING THE SUTTER CANAL

Chinese were the largest contingent of the two hundred workers hired by the Sutter Canal & Mining Company in 1870. The company planned to extend a canal that conveyed water from the Mokelumne River to Jackson and other areas to the north. Chinese workers were involved in constructing twenty-four miles of ditch, including erecting dams and a

---

4   Payroll records in the Amador County Archives cover August 1871 to February 1878.

reservoir, and building a mile-long flume over a sheer rock face. Over one hundred and twenty Chinese workers were represented by labor contractor Ye [Ge] Lung who contracted with the company to supply, feed and pay the laborers. Acting as agent for the Chinese workers and cooks, he also hired a Chinese supervisor to oversee day-to-day work. The company paid $28 a month per laborer, $1.50 per day for blasters, plus payment for cooks to feed the men. From April of 1870 through February of 1871, Ye Lung kept careful records of hours worked and receipts for payment in gold coin that he dispensed to his workers. However, by March the Sutter Canal & Mining Company's plans to extend the canal north ran into unanticipated problems and exorbitant costs. Defaulting under a new contract with Ye Lung, the company did not pay wages from March 1871 through August of 1871. On September 18, 1871, Ye Lung filed a lien in District Court to collect $10,663 owed to his workforce. Ye Lung testified in English and clearly documented what had been paid and what was owed. That lien, as well as other defaults, ultimately led to the bankruptcy of the Sutter Canal & Mining Company.[5]

ANTI-CHINESE ACTIONS

Anti-Chinese sentiments, which had been prevalent since the 1850s, gained momentum in the 1870s. In particular, laborers in San Francisco targeted Chinese workers as the cause of the economic crisis. Indicative of the conflict between unemployed labor and wealthy employers who hired Chinese workers, an April 1, 1876 editorial in the *Amador Ledger* stated, "So far the white laboring classes have been the only sufferers by the presence of the Chinese. The manufacturers and capitalists have found it to their advantage to employ this Coolie labor. Whenever the pockets of merchants and capitalists are made to suffer from the Chinese, it will not be long before something is done to abate the nuisance." The article was entitled, *The Mongolian Curse*. The slogan "The Chinese Must Go," first used by the Workingmens' Party in San Francisco, was heard throughout California. Chinese were accused in the press and by politicians of being heathens, instilling vice, working for low wages and taking jobs away from Americans.

In Sutter Creek, which lacked a separate Chinese section, one hundred and thirty workingmen held an anti-Chinese meeting in April 1876.

5 Amador County District Court, 11th Judicial District, Yee Lung, vs. Sutter Canal & Mining Company, E. Ginocchio, etc., "Deposition for Proof of Debt No. 1, Claim of Ye Lung," and Cenotto, *Logan's Alley*, vol.4, pgs. 220-272.

In May, the city of Jackson held a similar meeting in which attendees resolved to discourage whites from employing Chinese, trading with Chinese, and selling them tracts of land for mining purposes. In June the Order of Caucasians was formed in Sutter Creek, one of fifty-six chapters in California. Anti-Chinese petitions were circulated in Amador County at the end of 1877 in the towns of Amador City, Sutter Creek, Jackson and Plymouth and turned in to the Order of Caucasians in the farming town of Chico on the northeast edge of the Sacramento Valley, where violent actions against the Chinese were taking place.[6]

Resistance by Chinese

The *Amador Ledger* reported several incidents of harassment, such as "hoodlums of Sutter Creek stoning any inoffensive Chinaman who happens to put in an appearance on the streets" in the October 17, 1876 issue or "Cutting off a Chinaman's queue is the latest amusement invested by the hoodlums of Jackson," as reported on Jan, 26, 1878. Clearly, these deeds were perpetrated by the bullies of the towns. However, not all Chinese were hapless victims. In August 1877 a lone Chinese man walking in Sutter Creek was attacked by someone in a group who threw a stone. He defended himself by firing a gun into the crowd. More stones were met by a volley of shots. Fortunately nobody was injured. The *Ledger* reported, "The Chinese in this town are all well armed, and they have determined to protect themselves from the hoodlums."

Unfair treatment with tax collection was another occurrence that roused Chinese resistance. The Foreign Miners' tax was declared unconstitutional in 1870, but Amador County still had the unpopular road poll tax, levied on all male residents for road improvement. Tax Collector Mike Joy found himself in the middle of some skirmishes, reported in the *Amador Ledger*. On July 6, 1878, when he approached a few Chinese in Clinton, northeast of Jackson, one man "was far more disposed to fight than pay." Joy claimed that he had prevailed "after the hardest fought battle he ever had."

Two weeks later (July 20) Joy was involved in another fight in Jackson. Three or four Chinese men asserted that they had already paid the road tax. Asked for proof, they left to obtain evidence. One man returned with an 1877 receipt, which the tax collector refused to accept. A fight broke

6 Pfaelzer, Jean, *Driven Out: the Forgotten War Against Chinese Americans* (New York, Random House, 2007), pgs. 61-74 describe the outrages against the Chinese in Chico and Butte County.

out, ostensibly started by several outraged Chinese. Local whites joined in the melee to defend Joy. One Chinese man was badly wounded when an Italian named Louis Cardinale hit him over the head with a club; the tax collector then joined in pummeling the injured man with a rock. The man appeared to be seriously injured, "confined in a small Chinese den, where the heat is stifling, and the air impregnated with the fumes of tobacco and opium." Cardinale and tax collector Joy were arrested and given bail bond of $1,000 each. This sum was reduced several days later when the injured man appeared to be out of danger. The accused were nevertheless ordered to appear before a Grand Jury because agreement on a financial settlement was not reached with the victim.

Figure 21. Unidentified Chinese worker, Ione. *Amador County Archives*

MORE TROUBLES

An arson attempt to burn down Jackson's Chinatown in January 1878 was thwarted before it could be consumed by fire. The next month, on February 17, 1878, the destruction of Chinatown was accomplished by the implacable forces of nature. In less than two hours a deluge of rain swelled the north fork of Jackson Creek into a wall of water. It completely inundated Chinatown and some nearby properties built alongside the creek. Houses, stores and a huge oak tree were swept away in seconds. Seven people died in the flood. Apart from one white man, the rest of dead were Chinese; four men and two women were found stripped of clothing, some as far as twelve miles down river. Eight Chinese stores, with property estimated at $15,000, were lost. Property losses occurred elsewhere in Jackson when the middle fork of the river flooded, but the worst damage was to Chinatown.

In July 1878, the *Amador Ledger* correspondent for Plymouth reported, "Plymouth is entitled to be the banner town as far as the 'Chinese must go' question is concerned. Here we have no Chinese manufactories, wash houses, opium dens, or low gambling holes, nor yet houses of prostitution. As far as I can learn only three Johns are employed in the whole town. Good for Plymouth."

In 1879, California's second constitution reinforced discrimination against the Chinese by prohibiting the employment of Chinese by corporations and state, county or municipal governments.

The Legislature delegated "all necessary power to incorporated cities and towns of the State for the removal of Chinese...and it shall also provide the necessary legislation to prohibit the introduction into this State of Chinese after the adoption of this Constitution."[7]

---

7 California Constitution, Article XIX (1879) in http:/ faculty.lls.edu/manheim/cl1/ Chinese.

CHINESE EXCLUSION AND BOYCOTTS IN AMADOR COUNTY

CHINESE EXCLUSION ACT INTERPRETED LOCALLY

The anti-Chinese movement reached its zenith in the 1880s. Starting with California, pressure was put upon Congress to enact legislation to prevent Chinese laborers from immigrating to the U.S. This resulted in the Chinese Exclusion Act of 1882, banning skilled and unskilled laborers from entering the country for ten years. The only exceptions were merchants, as well as Chinese students, teachers, tourists and government officials who were few in number. Merchants were exempted because the U.S. continued to trade with China and did not want to endanger commerce. Worse, all Chinese were prevented from becoming U.S. citizens through naturalization. Such prejudiced legislation singled out the Chinese from any other race or ethnicity immigrating to the U.S. In 1888 the Scott Act extended Chinese exclusion for an additional ten years and prohibited reentry of all Chinese workers who had chosen to temporarily visit China. Many Chinese periodically made the voyage to China to visit their families. With this new legislation, about 20,000 laborers were not permitted to return to the U.S. This blocked their hopes for employment and residence in Gold Mountain, a land where they could potentially escape from the poverty of China and find new opportunity. The message was clear that Chinese were unwanted in the U.S.

"The Chinese question" regarding the Chinese presence in the U.S. played out in various ways in Amador County, influenced by state and national movements. The 1880 Census revealed that the largest Chinese population was in Ione and Lancha Plana (534), followed by the smaller towns of Fiddletown (134) and Volcano (105). Only 90 were listed for Jackson.

The city of Ione was not pleased with the results. The July 17, 1880 issue of the *Amador Ledger* reported:

> The most noticeable feature about these returns [Township 2] is the large proportion of Chinese, embracing 22 percent of the population. In no part of the county does the Mongolian element constitute anything like so formidable a part of the community....It will be a surprise to most of our readers to learn that the agricultural section of Amador is so heavily weighted with the Chinese curse. To account for their presence in such numbers, we are forced to conclude not merely that they form the bulk

of employees on the branch railroad and at the coal mines and gravel claims, but also that they are employed to a considerable extent on the ranches.

Indeed, several Chinese were listed on the Census as orchardists, fruit raisers, and farm workers. The newspaper published a letter from Ione a few days later on July 21 in which the author decried the lack of animation and vitality in both Ione and Lancha Plana. He attributed it to the large number of Chinese in the vicinity plying "their busy hands in the mines, orchards, gardens, and hop-yards of the neighborhood." In September of 1881 Lancha Plana's Chinatown was completely destroyed by fire. Although the cause was never confirmed, it may have been caused by the refilling of a burning coal oil lamp by a Chinese man who was subsequently seriously burnt.

CHINESE EXCLUSION ACT OF 1882

In April 1882, before the passage of the Exclusion Act, President Chester A. Arthur vetoed proposed legislation that would have stemmed Chinese immigration for twenty years. It was vetoed because of a potential conflict with a new treaty with China, which reaffirmed the right, privileges and immunities of Chinese people in the U.S., even as it allowed suspension, but not prohibition, of immigration of Chinese labor.

The veto did not sit well with the towns of Sutter Creek and Jackson. In Sutter Creek an effigy of the President was hung from a rope on Main Street, accompanied by a band playing a funeral dirge. Not to be outdone, Jackson did much the same in its business section, some protesters beating the effigy, and then setting it on fire. The *Amador Ledger* sympathized with the sentiment, but deplored "the barbarous usages of a couple of centuries back as the proper way of expressing disapproval."

A month later, President Arthur agreed to a ten-year immigration limit and signed the Chinese Exclusion Act, passed by Congress on May 6, 1882. Some of the Chinese of Amador County were angered, and possibly frightened, by the new anti-Chinese laws. The *Amador Dispatch* of May 13 reported on the reaction of Ione's population: "The Chinese residents of this place had a big jamboree in Chinatown last Saturday and Sunday, and we learn that the Ione Celestials had a monster blow out on Tuesday night. Whether they were celebrating the veto of the first Chinese bill or the signing of the new one...we were unable to find out." It is likely that the Chinese of Ione were protesting the passage of the Exclusion Act.

INTIMIDATION OF THE CHINESE

Chinese dominated the laundry business and operated "wash houses" in Jackson, Sutter Creek, and Ione. This was one profession open to Chinese where there was no competition. Still, there was vulnerability. In June of 1883 a Chinese laundry in Jackson was vandalized by bullies who cut clothing hanging on the outside line into small pieces. No complaint was filed. Two years later, several property owners tried to buy out Jackson's Chinese wash house in order to tear it down. Sutter Creek's Chinese laundry was similarly "suppressed," only to be rebuilt by the Chinese elsewhere in town.

A discriminatory hog pen ordinance was passed by the Amador County Board of Supervisors in July, 1883 aimed at relocating pigs raised in Chinatown. Many Chinese raised pigs both for their own consumption and for sale to others. Chinese were the first to comply, moving their pens from Jackson's Chinatown to a Chinese garden north of town.

The Chinese exclusion laws were not sufficient to quell anti-Chinese hostility. Lawless individuals continued to resort to arson as a method of getting rid of the Chinese. Fiddletown's Chinatown was destroyed by arson in September 1884, and a week later an attempt to torch Jackson's Chinatown failed, thanks to vigilant Chinese guarding the district. This scenario was replayed in other Chinese communities. Resilient Chinese rebuilt their Chinatowns nevertheless.

BOYCOTT OF CHINESE WORKERS

As if arson wasn't sufficient to intimidate the Chinese to flee from their businesses and residences, a tactic developed in the Sierra Nevada town of Truckee served as a model that was imitated by other California towns. Truckee had already used arson and violence to terrify and discourage Chinese living and working in its vicinity, many of whom had worked on building the railroad. Chinese haters, provoked by Charles McGlashan, an ambitious newspaper editor, embarked on a mission to deprive hard-working Chinese of their livelihood by boycotting their businesses and firing them from jobs, essentially starving them out. The Truckee method was construed as a lawful way to expel the Chinese.[1]

---

1 For more discussion, see Pfaelzer, *Driven Out*, chapter 5, "The Truckee Method," pgs 167-197.

The pros and cons of a Chinese boycott were debated in Amador County during the first few months of 1886. The *Ione Valley Echo* supported the boycott in a March 13 editorial:

> We fail to see wherein boycotting is any way unlawful. Surely, a citizen has a right to say, 'I will not employ Chinese labor and I will not purchase Chinese made goods. I will not patronize those who employ Chinese, nor those who persist in dealing in Chinese made goods.'

The *Amador Ledger* chastised the *Echo* and took a strong stand against the boycott. Its March 16 editorial stated:

> We have always been opposed to the influx of this alien race; but we decline to chime in with a popular clamor, because it is popular; we refuse to sanction anti-Chinese methods, which if pursued, mean the actual starvation of 80,000 human beings in the land that is sacredly dedicated to freedom and human rights....We want it distinctly understood that the *Ledger*, while deploring the presence of the Chinese in such large numbers on this coast, is opposed to the boycotting business as a legitimate means to try to get rid of them. We recognize the right of every man to trade with and employ whom he pleases.

Anti-Chinese associations that formed in Ione and Plymouth pledged to use legal means to discourage the employment of Chinese labor and "to accomplish the legitimate removal of their presence from the community."

In Jackson, a public meeting was held in late March to discuss "the Chinese question." The meeting was largely influenced by prominent citizen and state assemblyman Anthony Caminetti[2], who had recently attended the Sacramento Anti-Chinese Convention which advocated cessation of Chinese immigration, removal of Chinese "by every lawful measure" and statewide boycotts of Chinese labor.[3] Both Caminetti and Charles McGlashan of Truckee served on the Executive Committee as delegates-at-large, along with representatives from each county in the State.

---

2 Anthony Caminetti was elected to the California State Assembly in 1883, the California State Senate in 1886, the United States Congress in 1890 and re-elected to the State Assembly 1896 and 1898.

3 The platform of the convention, reproduced in full in the *Daily Alta California* on March 13, 1886, was overtly against the Chinese race and stated that the Chinese presence was "an invasion, not an immigration," that Chinese could not assimilate, had no families in California, and were antagonistic to a republican form of government "by education and customs." Chinese were also faulted for saving money that they sent back to China instead of spending locally.

Caminetti explained that the boycott entailed approaching businesses that employed Chinese and urging them to hire white workers in their place. Those who resisted the substitution would be boycotted. Not all at the Jackson meeting were in favor of taking these measures, declaring that they hampered the freedom of choice. Nonetheless, the Sacramento convention's platform was adopted. In April the Anti-Chinese Association's membership had increased from thirty-three to fifty-four, not a big turnout from a total of 2,140 white people residing in the Jackson township.

Initially, the enthusiasm for the boycott was high. The *Ione Valley Echo* triumphantly claimed on April 10 that, "Today, there is not, as far as we know, a Chinese cook, servant, or day laborer employed in town, except by their own people." The paper advocated closing the laundries, while observing "not enough white people can be found at present to do the work, and in consequence many of our citizens are forced, against their wishes, to give their washing to the Chinamen."

Within a few months, the boycott effort had fizzled out. By the end of May, the Plymouth Anti-Chinese Association disbanded. Plymouth was always the first to form an anti-Chinese organization despite the fact that there were few Chinese employed in Plymouth to start with. Ione's anti-Chinese organization, which had been so vocal about firing Chinese workers, was reported as apathetic.

The *Amador Ledger* proclaimed on June 19 that the Chinese cooks discharged from Ione's hotels had been rehired. "Indeed, the necessity of employment of Chinese cooks, under the circumstances, seems to be conceded. This state of things is to be deplored. White cooks have been so long banished from hotel kitchens that they are not able to perform the amount of work which a Chinaman accustomed to the work can get through with ease. This cannot be construed into an argument in favor of Chinese over white cooks."

The Jackson Anti-Chinese Association also disbanded. The boycott of Chinese labor was a failure in Amador County. Chinese labor was needed to perform work that whites didn't want to do.

THE FIDDLETOWN
EXCEPTION

FIDDLETOWN'S CHINESE POPULATION: THE 1870S

Fiddletown did not have an anti-Chinese association, perhaps because a third of its population was Chinese. Still, some white employers boycotted Chinese labor. In late 1877, the American Flat Gravel Company bought out most of the claims in the area, making it the largest mining enterprise. The company's new owners declared that there was only one Chinese worker out of seventy employees.[1]

The town grew slightly from the previous decade to total 1,200 people, but it was not in the county mainstream where the deep-shaft quartz mines existed. Fiddletown's commercial section was still lively; farming and mining were the major occupations of the residents in the greater vicinity.

As in the previous decade, miners made up the preponderance of Chinese immigrants (80 percent), most working independently or with their own companies since white employers did not want to hire them. The 1870 Census includes a few people with other occupations than mining: merchants Wo Sing [Sing Wo], age 43; On Yee, age 25; Foo Kee, age 47; and Ah Hon, age 30. All of these merchants had Chinese clerks working in their stores. Among other residents, Cheong Fu was a cook in a restaurant, Ah Hin a tailor, Ah Hunn a physician, Ah Choyn a doctor, Ah Lung a baker, Chung a barber, and Ah Lim and Ah Hu, were lottery dealers. The Census also lists thirty-seven Chinese women, "keeping house," still few compared to the number men.

Hard as life might have been for Chinese miners, laborers and other workers, there was still hope for betterment in the U.S. As occurred in other Chinese communities, letters went back and forth between Fiddletown and the home villages; friends returned to China with news about success in Gold Mountain. Those who could afford it periodically returned to China temporarily to visit family or marry and beget children, preferably sons. Others who had acquired wealth in California (mostly merchants) made the journey back home to China and contributed to the improvement of their families and villages. Chinese immigrants continued to journey to California, joining relatives and others who had settled in Fiddletown and elsewhere. Many were looking for work since economic conditions in Guangdong continued to be dire.

---

1 *Amador Ledger*, December 15, 1877.

It appears from records that Fiddletown's Chinese population in 1870 consisted of people from several districts of the Pearl River Delta region in southeast China.[2] The more prosperous counties of the Sam Yup district, where many merchants originated from, were well represented in Fiddletown. Immigrants from the Sze Yup district, especially Toishan County, were also present. Those from this area, mostly farmers and laborers, spoke a dialect known as Toishanese. In addition, Fiddletown's Chinese population included some people from the county of Heungshan. Though the Chinese residents in town may have spoken different dialects, they were all viewed as Chinese by Americans. Perhaps business and friendship transcended their place of origin and they mingled together. As will be seen, the entire Chinese community was involved in raising funds for the town cemetery.

Figure 22. Fiddletown looking west late 1800s. *Amador County Archives*

2 Fiddletown's *Cemetery Record Book* and the *Fiddletown Burial Book*, discussed in the chapters "Fiddletown's Chinese Chinese Cemetery" and "Burial in Fiddletown, Return to China" give origins of Chinese residents.

FIDDLETOWN CHINATOWN UNDER PRESSURE

In the 1880s Fiddletown was known as a Chinese town. At least 46 percent of its population was Chinese, more likely half of the town. About 15 percent of Fiddletown's Chinese population consisted of women and girls. The merchant Chew Kee came into prominence during this decade, joined by his wife Sigh Choy. The town itself had contracted in size to become a village of about 300 people. It even had a new name—*Oleta*, as it was called from 1878 until 1932. The active commercial section on Main Street, including Chinatown, encompassed merchandise stores, livery stables, blacksmith shops, hotels, boarding houses, saloons, a brewery, an opium den, and gambling house.

THE KUTCHENTHAL MURDER

Interchange between the two sections of town became apparent in the search for perpetrators after a brutal murder occurred. On the morning of January 26, 1881, Henry Augustus Kutchenthal, a clerk in a merchandise store in the center of Main Street, was found dead in a pool of blood with several wounds to his head. The murder weapon was an axe or hatchet belonging to the store. Footprints leading from the front and back doors confirmed that at least two people were involved in the crime. Neither money nor valuables were missing from the store, nor were strangers observed in town on the night of the murder.

Although the motive of the crime was baffling, the first to be suspected were Fiddletown's Chinese people. The *Amador Ledger* reported on January 29, "Oleta possesses in proportion to its population, a larger Chinese element than any other town in the county. Much of the business done by Kutchenthal was with this Chinese population. They were in the habit of selling their gold dust to him, and getting their goods from him. This dealing in gold frequently led to his having large sums of money in the store...."

Chinatown was thoroughly searched by the sheriff. In mid-February, one Chinese man was arrested on flimsy grounds. Again from the *Amador Ledger*, "When the murder was discovered, there was a half-gallon measure half full of China brandy, standing under the faucet, conveying the impression that liquor had something to do with the deed. This, however, is not regarded as a sure sign that the murderers are Chinamen,

79

as white men indulge in that low class of spirits." The arrested Chinese man was not involved, but liquor was. The case was not solved until September, 1883 when a local boy from a well-known family confessed to being a party in the crime. He and two others were arrested, none of them Chinese. The crime had occurred when one of the accused tried to steal liquor from the store and was confronted by the unfortunate Mr. Kutchenthal.

In 1880, about half of the Chinese residents were miners. Mining in Fiddletown was not thriving at the time, although over fifty Chinese were employed by local owners of small mining operations; when mining slowed down, they lost their jobs. Independent placer mining could be more remunerative. In 1883, a company of Chinese men working near American Flat, a historically rich site, obtained several thousand dollars worth of gold from land they purchased for $300.

REACTION TO THE EXCLUSION ACT AND REPERCUSSIONS

The chilling effect of the Chinese Exclusion Act of 1882 echoed in Fiddletown. According to one news report, the Chinese were arming in Amador County. In Fiddletown (Oleta) specifically, "a company, armed with rifles, and consisting of about fifty, drill regularly and practice marksmanship. As soon as one of any number of the company have attained a standard of proficiency, they are replaced by raw recruits."[1] Were the Chinese of Fiddletown organizing resistance to the Exclusion Act or was the press whipping up fear among whites?

The source of the information is questionable, coming from a new one-sheet newspaper called the *Plymouth Reporter*, first making its appearance in mid-April 1882. Plymouth was notoriously anti-Chinese, yet this news was picked up by the *Sacramento Daily Union*, which stated, "This may seem a little sensational, but it is no careless assertion. We get our information from reliable authority." However, none of the local Amador County newspapers reported on armed resistance in Fiddletown.[2]

There is a good possibility that the Chinese in Fiddletown were preparing to defend themselves against any violence by white vigilantes. Many must have been disheartened and discouraged by the passage of the Chinese Exclusion Act. In July, 1882, a few months after the legislation

1   *Sacramento Daily Union*, May 10, 1882.
2   Pfalzer. *Driven Out*, pg. 260 credits Amador County Chinese of forming an armed militia of fifty in protest.

Figure 23. Fiddletown remained rural and small. *Amador County Archives*

was passed, a "two-horse load" of Chinese left Fidddletown and started for China, leaving behind hopes of settling in California.

Disaster came to Fiddletown's Chinatown in September 1884 from arson, a tactic employed to destroy other Chinatowns. Fiddletown was one of the few towns in Amador County that had not been consumed by a major fire. J.D. Mason observed in his 1881 history of Amador County that the Chinese owned most of the older part of town. He observed, "The buildings, water worn and sunburned, would burn up in a moment if a fire were once kindled, and the old landmarks would be gone."[3] This was a portent of sorts, because three years after this was written, an arsonist torched and destroyed Chinatown in the "largest blaze that Oleta has even seen."[4] All the wooden buildings were burned, about twenty-five of them including three or four stores. Around two to three hundred people were left homeless. The fire was confined to Chinatown, kept from spreading eastward by efforts to save the livery stable at the border of Chinatown.

By January 1885 Chinatown had been rebuilt. Charles Atkinson, the owner of the livery stable located at the eastern border of Chinatown, purchased a few lots below his stable for protection in case of future attempts to set the Chinese section on fire. Curiously, there was no

---

3 [Mason, Jesse D.] *History of Amador County, California*, pg. 225.
4 *Amador Ledger*, September 6, 1884.

mention in the newspapers regarding the brick structures that survived the fire—the Chew Kee Store, the gambling house opposite, and the Foo Kee General Store to the east.

During the boycott of Chinese labor in 1886, Fiddletown became a refuge for Chinese fleeing the effects of discrimination. The February 22 edition of the *Amador Ledger* observed that as a result of the boycott Chinese from other areas were gravitating to Amador County. "This increase is noticeable in towns where the Chinese have always been strong. In Oleta and Ione, the Chinese inhabitants have increased in number so as to draw attention." Fiddletown's close-knit Chinese community provided safety and shelter.

DAILY LIFE ON GOLD MOUNTAIN

A WEB OF CONNECTIONS: Chinese Associations

Chinese arriving in California and the U.S. were closely tied to countrymen coming from the same area in southeast China. Their place of origin in China was the framework for relationships within their community as well as their source of identity in a strange inhospitable country. For support and sustenance they sought out others from the same county in Guangdong Province (with Guanzhou as the capital)—people who spoke the same dialect and perhaps knew their relatives back in the home villages.

District associations

Much like the penchant of Americans for establishing social, civic and charitable clubs, Chinese immigrants formed an intricate web of benevolent associations that linked immigrants to each other. As mentioned earlier, district associations or *huiguans*, were essential to sustaining, aiding and caring for Chinese immigrants from entry to California until departure for China. The district associations aimed at mediating disputes, protecting their members from anti-Chinese violence and assisting the needy and elderly to return to China. They brokered arrangements for the return home, issuing exit permits after debts were settled and fees were paid. Their "departure certificate" (*chut gong piu*) was required before the ship could be boarded. Through affiliate organizations, these district associations also took responsibility for exhuming the bones of the dead and transporting them to China.

By 1851 merchants formed two major district associations—the *Sam Yup Association* (Sanyi Huiguan) representing the three counties around Canton (Namhoi, Punyu and Shunduk) and the *Sze Yup Association* (Siyi Huiguan) representing four counties west of the Pearl River Delta (Sunning later called Toishan, Hoiping, Yunping and Sunwui). In addition, other districts in Guangdong formed their own organizations. The larger associations frequently fragmented into smaller units having some commonality between members, such as belonging to a single county or clans with the same surname. There was not necessarily cooperation among these groups and feuds did break out between them.

One such feud came close to becoming violent in Jackson at the end of May 1854. Two large opposing contingents of Chinese men began to gather and arm themselves for a violent confrontation. The newspaper hypothesized that the conflict involved disagreement between Canton and Hong Kong factions over a policy in China that affected them in California. More likely, the clash occurred over some internal disagreement between members of two district associations, possibly the Sze Yup Association and the Sam Yup Association. What raised alarm in the county was a wagon filled with "warlike implements of the "queerest manufacture possible," including long poles with knife blades stuck at the ends, and small short swords. A Chinese man representing one of the groups was reported to be purchasing steel in Stockton for making steel pikes. Fortunately, the "war" never took place; the weapons were seized by the sheriff and the instigators were arrested on June 1.[1]

In the town of Weaverville far to the northwest of Amador County, a similar conflict which resulted in violence broke out in June of that same year. Known as the Weaverville War," this clash also involved a dispute between members of different associations, also mistakenly identified as Cantons against Hong Kong. Four different associations were present in Weaverville, including those representing Sam Yup and Sze Yup. One group accused the other of cheating in the Chinese gambling house. In the ensuing battle, which became known as the "Weaverville War," eight people were killed and twenty wounded.

The Sam Yup Association in Fiddletown: the Chong How Benevolent Association

The Sam Yup Association, with headquarters in San Francisco, had branches as early as 1850 in Stockton and 1851 in Sacramento with the object of looking after the interests of the Chinese who gravitated to the mining areas.

This association had a distinct presence in Fiddletown. Many of the town's merchants and entrepreneurs originated from Punyu County. An affiliate organization associated with people from this county, the *Chong How Benevolent Association* (Changhou Tang), was well represented in Fiddletown. When deeds to the town were first awarded in 1871, a man called Ah Chow procured land on behalf of the Chong How Association. Unlike other properties obtained by Chinese residents, this parcel was not on Main Street. It was on a small side street north of town, now called

1 *Sacramento Daily Union*, May 29 and June 1, 1854 obtained information about the feud from the *Calaveras Chronicle* and the *San Joaquin Republic.*

Fiddletown Street. Years later, in 1909 and 1912, tax records showed that the organization was still present but in another part of town, probably on Main Street.

The purpose of the Chong How Association was to exhume and return the bones of the deceased to China for burial in their native villages. More on this custom will be described in the chapter *Burial in Fiddletown, Return to China*. What is significant is that rare and detailed records of the Chong How Association, giving the history of shipping thousands of bones from San Francisco to Hong Kong, have been found in the Chew Kee Store.

THE CHEW YEE TONG

Chinese immigrants also formed other organizations referred to as *tongs*, translated as "meeting hall" in Chinese, but also known as secret societies. In California some tongs were formed to protect Chinese from pervasive violence, but others which became quite notorious were involved in illegal and criminal activities, including gambling, prostitution and importing of opium.

The *Chew Yee Tong* (Chaoyi Gongsuo) was yet another affiliate organization of the Sam Yup Association. This was organized by the Punyu people in San Francisco in the late 1880s during a time of fierce conflict between the district organizations. The Chew Yee Tong's purpose was to protect Sam Yup and Chong How Benevolent Association members. In a similar manner to other immigrant organizations, conflicts in the home country were carried along by new arrivals and erupted in the new world setting. The Chew Yee Tong essentially functioned as a gang, involved in open wars with rival Chinese organizations. It also had a powerful influence over affiliates, whose members in other communities often contributed funds out of fear. Chinese in Fiddletown including merchant Chew Kee and Jimmie Chow contributed to this organization.

CHINESE MASONIC LODGE IN JACKSON

The Chinese Masonic Lodge in Jackson was organized on August 7, 1879 and located on north Main Street in Jackson's Chinatown. Many chapters of the Chinese Masons were formed in the 1870s in California and elsewhere in the U.S and Canada. The organization was not in any way affiliated with the Freemasons and its only similarity was that it

Figure 24. Jackson Masonic building. *Amador County Archives*

enacted elaborate rituals for members. The Chinese have a long history of anti-Imperial secret societies. Many secret societies organized in China by the predominant Han Chinese tried unsuccessfully to drive out the ruling Manchurian rulers with rebellions and uprisings. The Chinese Masons followed in this tradition, adopting the goal in the nineteenth century of overthrowing the unpopular Qing Dynasty.[2] Perhaps the name *Masons* gave the organization some sort of legitimacy in the eyes of the white population because of easy name recognition.

In the 1880s the name of the organization was changed from Chinese Masons to the *Chi Gung Tong* or *Chee Kung Tong* (Zhigongtang), adopted by the Chinese in Jackson. The Chi Gung Tong became increasingly powerful, possibly the most powerful Chinese organization abroad, also implicated in organized criminal activity. It gave support to Dr. Sun Yatsen, (Sun Yixian) who joined the Honolulu chapter in 1904 to gain help in funding and promoting the Chinese revolution.

In 1880, a big celebration occurred in Jackson's Chinatown to commemorate the opening of the Chinese Masonic Hall. The *Amador Dispatch* of July 17, 1880 described the festivities:

A Big Celestial Pow-wow—The Chinese have just completed a new building in the lower end of town, which is ornamented on the inside

2   This organization was preceded in mid-eighteenth century China by the Heaven and Earth Organization (*Tien Di Hui*), which initially acted as an association for poor migrants, but was later involved in local uprisings and criminal activity. More about its origins and eventual anti-Manchu stance is elaborated in http://freemasonry.bcy.ca/history/chinese_freemasons/index.html.

with a number of curious looking characters and images, and which we are informed is to be used as a Masonic hall or temple. In honor of the completion of this temple a large number of Chinamen from Drytown and other places assembled here last Saturday and commenced raising the most unearthly racket we ever heard, at the same time producing and flourishing in the street one of the most hideous looking images that could well be pictured out by the most fertile imagination of any human being.... The flourishing of this thing through the streets was kept up at intervals until Sunday night, accompanied by the melodious strains of a full fledged Chinese band...It is generally presumed that the great pow-wow was intended as a sort of dedicatory ceremony for the new building.

Spectators and participants watched the rollicking and joyful lion dance where the huge stylized papier-mâché head and colorful layered-cloth body of the beast paraded through the streets borne by several dancers in constant motion. In front of the lion, a smiling big- headed Buddha holding a fan led the way. Celebratory lion dances were performed for special occasions, a tradition that carries forward to the present.

From this description, the Jackson Masonic Lodge opening attracted Chinese from other communities besides residents in Jackson's Chinatown. Whether or not the Jackson branch activities were primarily political or social or possibly gang-related (as occurred elsewhere) is not known. The local organization was known as prosperous and powerful.

CHARITABLE CONTRIBUTIONS IN THE CHINESE COMMUNITY

Concern for the poor is a feature of Chinese culture where the less fortunate are often the recipients of aid and offerings of food. In Gold Mountain, Chinese organizations solicited donations for the poor and needy, for maintenance of temples and cemeteries, for religious ceremonies and for their own continuance. Fiddletown's Chinese community, including women, actively donated to various charities. Books requesting donations for different causes were distributed by parent organizations in San Francisco to local merchants, to be displayed in their stores. Visitors to the store were encouraged to contribute and add their names and native county to a list of donors from other areas. The books discovered in the Chew Kee Store demonstrate links among the various Sam Yup organizations:

- An 1882 account book of the Punyu organization that tracks income going in and out in Fiddletown. Contributors included merchants Foo Kee, Ngan Chew Kee, and a man of means named Ga Gum Yuk.
- An 1888 book soliciting donations for Sacramento's annual ceremony for the deceased who were unclaimed by relatives.
- An 1895 book from San Francisco's Chew Yee Tong asking for contributions from Punyu people. Ngan Chew Kee and Ga Gum Yuk donated money to this cause.
- An 1899 book soliciting funds for the Sam Yup Temple in San Francisco. There were four donors from Punyu, three with the last name of Ngan (from the same clan, not necessarily from the same family).

These books from the Chew Kee Store demonstrate the connections within and between the Chinese communities, spanning from San Francisco to distant mining towns. Despite prevalent anti-Chinese legislation and actions, the Chinese looked after each other, and those in Fiddletown were generous to their fellow countrymen.

CHINESE WOMEN, MEN AND LIVING ARRANGEMENTS

CHINESE WOMEN

Few Chinese women voluntarily came to California. Tradition kept women in their village, close to their families or in-laws. The journey to America was expensive and life in California was filled with hardships. It made more economic sense for men coming to the U.S. to send their earnings home where the money could be stretched farther to help the entire family.

Some families in China were so desperately poor that they sold their daughters into prostitution or servitude and these girls became vulnerable to forcible passage to the U.S. Although in the early 1850s a few Chinese prostitutes came voluntarily to California, by 1854 Chinese tongs had taken control of the prostitution trade. Girls and young women were imported by the tongs, procured by kidnapping or under false pretenses of marriage or work as servants. Some known as *mui tsai* were sold to well-off Chinese families who treated them as property. These women lived as virtual slaves. Others were forced into prostitution or indentured servitude. Many were sent to the mining areas, where there was a dearth of women and, consequently, money to be made.

From early on, Chinese prostitutes were present in Amador County, and their customers were surely not just the Chinese. In 1854 a female resident of Fiddletown involved in the church and Sons of Temperance decried the presence of "Chinese and other prostitutes, who have been driven from the cities." Six Chinese "women of pleasure" were counted in the 1860 Census for Fiddletown. They ranged in age from eighteen to thirty years and lived in the same house as a gambler, Ah Lang, age thirty.

The Jackson town council was indicted in 1855 by the Grand Jury for obtaining money under false pretenses by levying a monthly license tax of $20.00 on "Chinese houses, thereby meaning and intending houses of ill fame kept for purposes of public prostitution and occupied by Chinese whores." About $2,000 had been collected from various brothels, including one owned by P.P. Rozario, who held quite a bit of property in Jackson's Chinatown. The tax was deemed illegal by the Grand Jury. Yet, the following term, charges were dismissed against the council, and houses of prostitution continued to be a feature of Jackson life until the mid-twentieth century.

The life of a prostitute was desperate, as can be seen from an 1873 inquest in Drytown into the death from opium poisoning of a Chinese woman named Ah Choy. She was observed eating opium mixed with water, crying out in distress several hours later. The reasons why Ah Choy consumed the opium were contested. According to the testimony of one Chinese witness, she was not a user of opium. This person claimed that she was forced to eat the opium by Ah Man, whom she refused to marry. Ah Man's testimony was just the opposite, claiming that she took her life because she did not want to live in a brothel and raise money for marriage to him through prostitution. The inquest panel concluded that she committed suicide, a fate that befell many women forced into prostitution. In China, swallowing opium was commonly used by prostitutes as a method to end their lives. Ah Choy was about twenty-years-old and chose this form of death as preferable to living as a prostitute.

Not all Chinese women in Amador County were prostitutes. Some Chinese women worked and lived in other capacities; for instance one woman in 1860 Drytown was a beekeeper, another worked as a washerwoman. Several women in the Jackson area described themselves as laborers in the 1860 Census.

A few recorded marriages were performed between Chinese men and women. The earliest took place in Jackson in 1854 between Assim and Ah Hou. Other documented weddings occurred in Drytown, Lancha Plana, and Fiddletown. In 1860, Ah Look of Camache, age twenty-nine, was joined in marriage to Ah Gee from San Francisco, age nineteen. Both were originally from Guangzhou. That same year in Drytown, Ah Hung, age twenty-five wedded Ah How, age twenty. Three marriages were recorded for Fiddletown residents: Ah Poo and Ming Sing in 1863, Ah Pokiman and Len Qui in 1867, and Wong Cun and Foak Thoy in 1880. There were undoubtedly other unions that were never officially recorded.

The Page Act in 1875 aimed at barring Asian prostitutes from entering the U.S., making it difficult for *any* Chinese woman to gain entry. All Chinese women attempting to enter the U.S were suspected of being prostitutes, even those who were married or who made the voyage for other reasons. Coupled with the Chinese Exclusion Act of 1882, the number of women immigrating declined and remained proportionally small. This contrasts with the opportunity for settled family life in the

United States experienced by other groups of immigrants. Primarily wives of merchants, diplomats, Chinese students and U.S. citizens gained legal entry, and even they had to endure harassment from immigration officials. Most of the wives of merchants and upper-class Chinese were crippled by the custom of foot-binding, and they rarely left their homes, becoming an invisible presence in the American towns and cities where they resided.

In Amador County, as elsewhere in California, Chinese men greatly outnumbered women. In 1860 Drytown, which had the largest recorded number of Chinese, only 2 percent of the Chinese were women, numbering twelve. The same applied to Fiddletown. Jackson had the largest percentage of Chinese women to men in 1860, fifty-one out of 510 or 10 percent. The majority of these women were probably prostitutes. Much is unknown about the lives of the Chinese women who arrived here during the nineteenth century.

CHINESE MEN

Many of the tasks traditionally conducted by women—laundry, cooking, housekeeping—were performed in the U.S. by Chinese men, tasks they would never do in China. To survive, men would take on whatever work was available, especially as opportunities for employment dwindled with increasing hostility. Chinese cooks and servants often staffed hotels and households.

Figure 25. Men in Ione Chinatown. *Ken Clark*

Most Chinese men living in Amador County and elsewhere were deprived of the family life so important in China. Many had left their wives behind. For some, prostitutes were their only female contact. Prejudice, bolstered by a California 1872 anti-miscegenation law, prohibited interracial marriages. Discriminatory federal legislation resulted in fractured families. In the 1880s the Chinese Exclusion Act followed by the Scott Act banned Chinese laborers from entering the U.S. and kept laborers who had temporarily returned to China from reentering the country. Chinese men already earning a living in the U.S. (except for merchants) dared not return to China, becoming permanently estranged from their families. Many wives in China never saw their husbands again and were known as "Gold Mountain widows," some separated as long as twenty to thirty years. As the nineteenth century continued on, most of the Chinese men who stayed in California became de facto bachelors.

LIVING ARRANGEMENTS, CHILDREN

In the 1870 Fiddletown Census, women were 10 percent of the enumerated Chinese population. The profession for all of them was

Figure 26. Family man, possibly in Fiddletown. *Amador County Archives*

93

described as "keeping house," a term also applied to married Caucasian women who were housewives. But the living arrangements for most of the thirty-seven Chinese women were different than those of monogamous households, and one can only speculate that the majority of the women were prostitutes, especially since there were no children present; however, it is possible that some were relatives of men living in Gold Mountain. There were various combinations: three to five women, ranging in age from eighteen to forty, living with one man, usually a miner, or one to two women living with several miners, or some women-only residences consisting of two to four women, usually in their twenties. For example, Ah You, age thirty-one; Ah Qui, twenty-two; and Ah Koo twenty; lived with a Chinese miner, age forty-one. Another three women lived with Ah Soy, a cook. In one household, four women were keeping house with six miners. These were very different arrangements than existed with families in China, in which three or more generations lived under the same roof.

In other census listings, Ching, age twenty-one kept house with two miners, Ah Hip, thirty-two and Ah Foy, twenty-four. Ah Lin, a woman of forty years lived with Ah Kay, a thirty-year-old miner, the only documented example of a single female with a single male. Her age

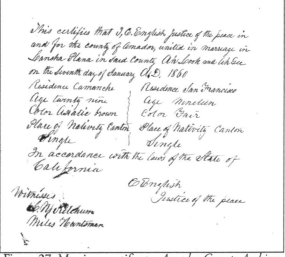

Figure 27. Marriage certificate. *Amador County Archives*

implies that she was a relative rather than a mate. Sing Choy, age thirty-two, stayed in the same quarters as the well-off merchant Foo Kee, age forty-seven, in addition to three clerks and a miner. She might have been a second wife or concubine.

There were also three different sets of women-only households, such as that of Ah You, age twenty-eight; Ah Choy, twenty-four; and Ah Hee, twenty-two; who lived together. These young women were certainly prostitutes. Yet they and other prostitutes were not looked down upon in Fiddletown where they fully participated in the Chinese community. These women had discretionary income for donating to charitable causes and for contributing to the money pool, as will be documented in the chapter on Fiddletown's Chinese Cemetery.

In Jackson by comparison, women composed 5 percent of the Chinese population and here, too the 1870 Census reveals few if any monogamous relationships. For example, four women were "keeping house" with thirty-four miners. The woman Vee Sun, age thirty-four was living with Ching Lang, a merchant, plus five miners, and twenty-one laborers. Since census takers went from household to household, it can be assumed that these living arrangements took place in boarding houses.

Jackson's census also identified the presence of Chinese children, born in California. For example, Ah Hee, age thirty, was keeping house with two children, age five and eight, plus two miners, and Ah Young, who was "in the family," possibly meaning a relative. Another woman, Ah Molly lived with Ah Sam, a washerman, and a three-year-old child, in addition to another woman Yu Sing, age thirty-five who was "in the family," and a miner, age thirty-eight. Could these have been traditional couples with children, even if the women were not identified as wives? In another case, three women were living together with a boy, age fifteen.

Yet ten years later in 1880, out of a total ninety Chinese who lived in Jackson, only twelve were women. Half were identified in the Census as "fancy women" of whom the youngest was fourteen and the oldest was age forty-five, quite an age range for prostitutes. They lived in a boarding house with forty-five people. The towns of Ione and Lancha Plana combined had only twenty-two Chinese women out of a much larger Chinese population of 534. Nine were listed as "fancy woman," with two others working in a "fancy store." The remainder of the female population was identified as wives and daughters.

By contrast, women's status had improved in Fiddletown by 1880. Although only twenty women out of the 136 Chinese were counted in the Census, most were recognized as wives, mistresses, and daughters. Some of these women may have been former prostitutes who had escaped or outlived their contracts; others may have been able to brave the difficult passage and immigration authorities to gain entry. One twenty-five-year-old woman, "Susie," lived alone and was identified as a mistress. Was she a prostitute, a madam, and/or a financially independent woman?

Fiddletown's Chinatown now contained two and three person households, often with a boarder or two. Some households included children, all identified as daughters, no sons listed. Despite all the obstacles, here was the beginning of family life. These children were born in California, and were entitled to U.S. citizenship after a Supreme Court ruling in 1898, denied to their China-born parents.

A storekeeper Ah Kee, age fifty, lived with his twenty-five-year-old wife and seven-year-old daughter. Ah Cho Kim, a forty-five-year-old wife, lived with her placer miner husband, age fifty, her daughter Ah Yee, age seven, and three boarders, one of whom was a woman. Ah Wung, a fifty-year-old pack man lived with his thirty-two-year-old wife and a fifteen-year-old boy, who worked in a store and is not identified as a son. The household of Ah Cho, a placer miner of fifty-four, consisted of his wife Mrs. Ah Cho, a ten-year-old daughter, Ah Ding, and a boarder, Mrs. Ah Ka Yow, age thirty-eight, described as "mistress."

Several women were wives or mistresses of gamblers, who made up 10 percent of Chinese men in Fiddletown. Ah He Toy, age twenty-eight, was the wife of a gambler Ah Sin, and also living with a placer miner. Ah Gwi, a thirty-five-year-old woman lived with Ah Lin, sixty-three who operated a gambling house. Of special note is a gambler, Ah Chu, forty-three-years-old, who lived with his wife Sarah, age thirty-four, in addition to a sixty-year-old boarder, a placer miner. Could the couple have been Chew Kee and Sigh Choy? The ages match exactly.

DIVERSIONS: OPIUM & GAMBLING

Both gambling and smoking opium provided entertainment, hope, and relaxation to hard working single men estranged from their families in China. Chinese immigrants did not introduce opium to the U.S. It was widely available in the 1800s as a patent medication, also in the form of laudanum, used for a variety of ailments as a painkiller and cough suppressant. Opium did not become illegal in the U.S. until 1909. The drug, already familiar to Chinese because of importation into China by the British, became a profitable export item for Hong Kong firms, which shipped cases of prepared opium to San Francisco. From there it was widely distributed by merchants to California's Chinese communities. Customers could always find boxes of opium in Chinese merchandise stores. The most popular and highest quality brand, *Lai Yuen*, was available in the Chew Kee Store, as were pipes and a lamp for heating the substance. *Lai Yuen* boxes, as well as those of other brands, were unearthed by archeologists in Drytown, along with opium pipe bowls and an opium needle.

Opium smoking was a communal activity among Chinese men, offering comfort and companionship after an exhausting day's work.

THE CHINESE GAMBLING HOUSE

Figure 28. Fiddletown Gambling House. *Ron Scofield*

97

It was also used as a medicine, soothing aching bodies. Producing a euphoric torpor, the drug was smoked in a variety of settings: gambling establishments, restaurants, association meeting places, and dens or places dedicated specifically to smoking the substance. It was smoked in brothels by clients and some prostitutes. Opium provided an escape from daily toil and alienation from American society. Not everybody who smoked became an incapacitated addict—most had to work the next day if they wanted to survive. However, there was always the risk of addiction. In China, opium addiction had a devastating effect on its nineteenth century society.

Public outcry in California began when white men and women were drawn to opium dens. At the time when anti-Chinese petitions were circulating in Sutter Creek, an article entitled "Degradations Depths," in the *Amador Ledger* of December 8, 1877 reported that members of the Order of Caucasians spied several men and women entering the Chinese den in that town to "seek the companionship of an alien race for the purpose of indulging in as filthy and debasing a practice as ever trapped our nature in its meshes…" Whites continued to frequent Sutter Creek's opium dens three years later despite efforts of self-righteous citizens to "ferret" them out. Chinese throughout the state were accused of smoking opium, and thereby associated with social vice.

Gambling had been pervasive among all ethnicities in California during gold rush days, even becoming licensed by the state and cities in 1850 as a way to raise money. But with the arrival of women and families anxious for respectability, the social milieu changed to overall disapproval of gambling. In 1860, banking games in which the player bets against the house were banned in California. Whereas propriety put a damper on overt gambling among whites, it flourished among Chinese laborers far from home. Gambling houses existed in all the various Chinatowns, offering a form of recreation that attracted Chinese laborers, always in need of good luck and willing to take risks for the possibility of instant wealth. There were high expectations back in China that Gold Mountain adventurers would return home rich.

Fiddletown had its share of Chinese gamblers since the 1860s when twelve were counted in the Census. By 1880, 10 percent of the town's Chinese were involved in gambling and lottery dealing. Chinese bachelors patronized Fiddletown's gambling houses, where they could try to better their circumstances on games such as *pai gow* (Chinese dominoes), *fan tan* and *mah jong*.

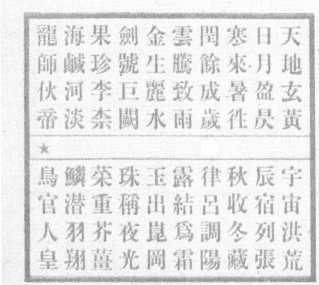

Figure 29. Lottery or "pigeon" ticket. *Sonia Ng*

Many Chinese bought lottery "pigeon tickets" from the Chew Kee Store. The tickets contained the Chinese characters for eighty unique words printed on a game sheet, and arranged in twenty poetic sentences, each consisting of four Chinese words. The words were derived from a well-known book in China, the *Thousand Character Classic*. Some of the four character poems are: "the sun and moon, full and waning;" "fall harvest, winter storage;" "gold inhabits graceful water;" "cold comes [winter], heat fades [summer]." Some of the words were poetically used nouns: "pearl," "dragon", "sword," "jade", "stars", etc. The game, called *Bak Gup Pil*, consisted of the player betting on several words, usually ten or more.[1]

Gamblers marked their selected characters on pigeon ticket lottery forms which were given to an agent, along with the money wagered. Runners and agents collected tickets from various establishments and recorded the bets before the drawing. At the appointed hour, usually in the evening, the "house" drew the winning words, each character written

---

1 Archeologist Jane Russell obtained translations of the one-character stamps used in the game, found in the Chew Kee Store. Examples of the four character poems and a description of *Bak Gup Pil* are taken from pg. 39-40 of her thesis, "An Ethnographic and Archaeological Examination of the Chew Kee (Store), Fiddletown, California." (Sacramento, California State University, 1991) and Stewart Cullin. "The Gambling Games of the Chinese in America," *Philology Literature and Archaeology*, Vol. 1, no. 4, 1891 reprinted. The gambling game *keno* is a derivative of *Bak Gup Pil*.

on a separate paper. The results were posted in stores, restaurants, and other establishments in the area. The more winning words (much like numbers) a person chose, the higher the take—minus a commission of up to 15 percent (5 percent for the house, 10 for the agent). Many hopes were placed on drawing a winning ticket. With a change in fortune, the winner could return from Gold Mountain to his village in China as a wealthy man and live a life of comfort and ease with his family. He could even become a benefactor to his family and his village.

Fan tan was especially popular in Chinese communities. Coins or small objects such as buttons were covered by a cup; players would place bets on how many would be left at the end after the objects were removed in units of four. A company of Chinese partners would organize the game, receiving a percentage of the winnings. Fan Tan was considered to be a banking game and thereby illegal. As anti-gambling laws were strengthened in the 1880s, Chinese gamblers and gambling houses were singled out in conjunction with the anti-Chinese movement.

Chinese gamblers were periodically arrested. For instance, in 1880 Ah Shung was arrested for playing fan tan in a rented house in Jackson. Others accused of gambling could receive heavy sentences in local courts. One man, fined $211 for gambling, was serving 105 days in county jail in lieu

Figure 30. Chops or stamps for lottery business. *D. Zorbas*

100

of payment. Three Chinese men arrested for gambling were each serving one year in jail. These cases were turned over to the Superior Court on writs of *habeas corpus* because such charges exceeded the authority of local courts.[2] In March of 1883, the local constable tried to close down Fiddletown's gambling house, mainly because it attracted white youth. The constable was also advised to investigate the local Chinese opium den.

Disputes and conflict could erupt over accusations of cheating and district rivalries. The March 27, 1886 *Ione Echo* newspaper reported a fight in Ione Chinatown that began with an accusation of cheating in a game of dominoes and ended with gun shots fired by members from two different associations, the See Yeh (Sze Yup) Company and the Young Wah Company. The person wounded was Ching Wo, who had made the accusation and belonged to the Sze Yup Association. Gambling, with all its side effects, was very much a part of life in Chinatowns in Amador County and elsewhere.

These forms of recreation among the Chinese became connected in the minds of Americans with dissolute and immoral behavior, providing fuel to the anti-Chinese movement. Prostitution was added to "Chinese vices" of opium smoking and gambling, even though brothels in Chinatowns were frequented by white men as well as Chinese. Yet in rowdy towns like Jackson, prostitution and gambling continued for years, long after the Chinese departed.

Figure 31. *Pai gow* tiles, drum, opium box. *Laura Faye Mah*

2 *Amador Ledger*, February 14, 1880 and December 18, 1880.

CHINESE CELEBRATIONS AND CUSTOMS TRANSPLANTED

CELEBRATIONS

Although Chinese immigrants mostly experienced a life of endless toil with little remuneration, there were occasions to celebrate. Three traditional major festivities were and still are always observed: Chinese New Year, the Dragon Boat Festival, and the Mid-Autumn Festival. The Chinese use a lunar calendar based on cycles of the moon, a different system than Western solar calendars, though also having twelve months. Special holidays are calculated by their relation to the lunar month (consisting of twenty-nine to thirty days); for example, the Mid-Autumn festival takes place on the fifteenth day of the eighth lunar month, around the time of the harvest moon in mid-September.

The most important and joyous festival is Chinese New Year, also known as the Spring Festival which occurs on the first day of the first new moon of the year, usually between January 21 and February 19, traditionally lasting for fifteen days. The holiday marks hope for good fortune and new beginnings, as the old is swept away and the new invited in with customs and foods that are highly symbolic. Both New Years Eve and New Years Day are family affairs in China, yet families were far away from the lonely men and women in California separated by an ocean from their relatives and ancestors. The district association or other affiliated organizations substituted for family.

Chinese New Year was celebrated in the various Chinatowns in Amador County with feasting and exploding firecrackers. In Fiddletown as reported in the *Amador Ledger* of January 22, 1881, "The Celestials—and we have a big camp of them—are making great preparations for their new year, which commences next Saturday. They have a heavy stock of chickens, etc. on hand for sacrifice." The Chinese in Fiddletown and other communities enjoyed special foods prepared for the holiday, sharing good wishes for the prized attributes of happiness, prosperity, longevity and fortune (fu). Stores and homes were decorated with the auspicious and lucky color red, which predominates in this holiday. Merchants distributed Chinese candy to neighborhood children.

The Chinese way of celebrating was raucous with gongs, drums and horns to frighten away evil spirits. Loud explosions of Chinese

Figure 32. Lion for festival dances. *D. Zorbas*

firecrackers echoed for years through the Chinatowns of Amador County. Even Plymouth, which did not have much of a Chinese population, reported, "China New Year is just booming at this place, firecrackers and bombs being exploded at all times of night."[1]

Another major holiday is the Dragon Boat Festival, occurring in June on the fifth day of the fifth lunar month, close to the summer solstice. The holiday is associated with the growth of rice in Southern China, and the river dragon is said to control the river flow and rainfall needed for a bountiful harvest. The Dragon Boat Festival originated as a tribute to the poet Qu Yuan (third century BC), whose sage advice was shunned by his ruler. He was banished from the kingdom and later drowned himself in the river after writing what became one of China's most famous elegies. In memory of the search for his body, the holiday features teams of rowers competing in an exciting race, their boats colorfully decorated as dragons.

Far from the ocean, the Dragon Boat Festival took a different form in Amador County. The *Amador Ledger* of July 24, 1880 reported on the festival in Jackson:

The Mongolians of Jackson held a sort of celebration this week—the first of the kind we have witnessed in the county. A couple of fires were

1 *Amador Ledger*, February 2, 1889. The bombs were called *Fa Pao*, meaning floral cannons

built on a vacant lot on Main Street, and a space of 20 yards or so was cleared to afford room for the leaders of the dance to operate in. At length the musicians appeared on the scene, the instruments consisting of the usual tin gongs that figure conspicuously in all Chinese concerts. Next the chief of the occasion appeared, and he was an object in himself. He bore a huge mask, representing a dragon, the tail of which was composed of a living Chinaman doubled up. The dance was kept up by the head and tail for about an hour on two evenings. It was quite a sample of endurance, and when over the performers were bathed in perspiration. The affair was witnessed by from 100 to 200 white spectators, who seemed quite interested in the antics of the heathen.

The dragon dance was both joyous and a test of stamina for the dancers crouched beneath the long and undulating body of the mock creature, as it weaved to and fro accompanied by loud music. Such Chinese celebrations both attracted and puzzled whites who gathered to see what was going on. At these festivals, Chinese from other nearby communities joined in, swelling the number of participants and onlookers at the event.

The third important festival, the Mid-Autumn Festival, celebrates the end of harvest, focusing on the large and brilliant harvest moon. Usually occurring around mid-September, it is also referred to as the Moon Festival, an occasion for honoring the moon and giving thanks for the

Figure 33. Chinese parade in Ione. *Amador County Archives*

harvest. Celebrants enjoy fruit, especially round fruit such as apples and melons, and round cakes known as *mooncakes*, all of which echo the full moon. In rural and agricultural Amador County, Chinese residents would have celebrated the end of harvest, a festive time for all the local people who were involved in growing fruit, vegetables and grain.

LANGUAGE AND NUMBERS

Cantonese, being a language of nine tones, has many words with similar sounds, provoking puns and wordplays that convey a cultural obsession with good and bad luck. For example, the word for *bat* in Chinese sounds like the word *fu* which means *luck*; pictorial and artistic depictions of bats therefore symbolically mean good luck. Similarly the word for *fish* in Chinese, *yu*, sounds like the word for *surplus*, evoked by both pictorial representations and serving fish during Chinese New Year. For that holiday, fresh fish, particularly carp (its name, *li*, has the same pronunciation as the Chinese word for *profit*), is prepared and eaten on the second day of New Year to extend profit into the coming year. Depictions of fish are used in many decorations, jewelry and paintings which convey its symbolic meaning.

This quality of spoken language carries over to numbers in China which are represented by different symbols than in the West. The Chinese numeral system is decimal (base-10). For example, 1 is represented by — and 10 is 十 and eleven is 十 — . The interpretation of numbers among the Chinese has special significance based on similarity of sounds to other words (homonyms) in the language. The number 3 connotes *live* or *birth* and is always welcomed, whereas the sound of the number 4 in Cantonese is similar to the word for *death*, thereby a number to be avoided. Other numbers have positive qualities: number 8 is associated with *prosperity* and *growth* because of its sounds and the number 9 connotes *long life*.

Numerology affected decisions and choices of Chinese immigrants. There were auspicious days for many of life's decisions, such as choosing dates for marriage, burial, starting a business, etc, and Chinese people consulted fortunetellers, almanacs, and the Chinese zodiac for guidance.

DEITIES AND TEMPLES

In China, religion encompasses a subtle and holistic combination of the ethical system of Confucianism, blended with Daoism, Buddhism, and regional folk beliefs. There are no special days like Sunday set aside for group worship or formal services, nor organized religion as known in the West—hence the labeling of Chinese immigrants as "heathens" by Westerners ignorant of Chinese culture. There is no single god but many deities, including *kuan yin*, the Buddhist goddess of mercy. The folk Kitchen God resides in household altars as guardian of the hearth, and is thanked and bidden farewell in a special ritual towards the end of every lunar year before ascending to heaven. Other deities embody different attributes, such as the three painted above the altar in the Chew Kee Store representing *fu* (fortune), *lu* (prosperity), and *shou* (longevity). The three deities are identified by holding symbolic items: a scroll for fortune, a scepter called a *ruyi* (everything as you wish) connoting prosperity, and peaches for a luxuriant and long life. Such symbolism is pervasive in Chinese culture.

Worship for Chinese immigrants was an individual endeavor, involving veneration of ancestors and appeal to favorite deities for guidance and help. The supplicant would give offerings of fresh fruit and flowers and would burn incense sticks (referred to as *joss sticks*) to send smoke upwards for communication with a deity or a deceased relative. In China, there were family altars in the home, but since Chinese migrants were far from home small altars were present in Chinese stores and organizations such as the Chi Gung Tong (Chinese Masons).[2] The Chinese also built temples in various communities. One of the most popular deities in temples and elsewhere was a famous Chinese general, *Guan Yu*, represented in statues or portraits with a red face and black beard. General Guan Yu, who died in 219 CE, played a major role in a civil war that led to the collapse of the Han Dynasty and is revered for his loyalty and valor. His image is still present in many temples and altars throughout modern China.

Jackson's Chinese temple was referred to as a "joss house," a term purportedly derived from the Portuguese word *deus*, meaning god. In general, Chinese temples throughout the West were referred to as joss houses. Jackson's joss house was located in Chinatown directly south of the north fork of Jackson Creek, next to a lot with a stone fence called "China Graveyard." Both properties were purchased separately by the Tung Wah Gee Shaw Company (also spelled on deeds as Tung Wa Yee Chow Co.), the graveyard lot bought in 1876 and the "old joss house"

---

2 The altar of the Chi Gung Tong was devoted to the founders of the Heaven and Earth Organization (*Tien Di Hui*), who were worshipped by members as deities.

in 1878. This was a joint company from San Francisco that might have taken over operation of the temple and graveyard. Temples were usually financed by wealthy families or benevolent associations. The Jackson joss house is shown on the 1890 and 1898 Sanborn Insurance maps. Later maps show the Chinese graveyard in a different location to the east of the commercial section, close to the public graveyard. Unfortunately no photographs or other information about the Jackson joss house have been uncovered. The fact that it was referred to as "old" in 1878 indicates that it might have been built decades earlier.

Another Chinese building in Jackson was referred to in English as the Chinese Church. On the photograph shown, the name in Chinese is translated as *Dung Wa*, denoting a charity house usually related to burial.

Figure 34. Chinese Church in Jackson. *Amador County Archives*

Its purpose may have been philanthropic, perhaps raising funds for the burial of poor miners and workers. It was established on August 7, 1879,

Figure 35. Chinese Joss House New Chicago. *Amador County Archives*

the same date that the Chi Gung Tong was organized in Jackson. There may have been connection between these two entities, which resemble each other in photographs. The Chinese Church property, in a different location with a different deed than the joss house had initially been purchased in 1870 by Ah Chin for the Nun Fun Co. The parcel is quite large and located several lots north of Chinatown.

Only one photograph remains of a beautiful Chinese temple identified as being above Drytown, in a mining area called New Chicago. Other than the photograph, nothing is known about this temple. The location seems unlikely, unless this was built before New Chicago became a mining community around 1878. Its exterior resembles a Chinese temple in Weaverville, far to the northwest, which is ornately furnished with much red and gold. That temple has three separate "spirit" houses or intricately carved wooden alcoves containing clay statues of male and female deities, and a long carved and decorated altar table for supplicants to give offerings and appeal to ancestors or a deity. Chinese temples were more elaborate than store or family altars, although their function was the same as far as communication with the deceased or divine entities. A temple attendant, not a priest, looked after the temple, and was available to tell a person's fortune for a fee by using divination sticks. It required wealthy individuals and a generous Chinese community to support such a temple. This seems unlikely in Drytown; building and maintaining such a temple would have required countywide support.

DEATH, FUNERALS AND THE AFTERLIFE

Death is perhaps the greatest mystery of human existence. Humans throughout the millennia have grappled with these questions: Why do we die? What is the purpose of our lives? What happens after we die? Is there an afterlife? Is good behavior rewarded and bad behavior punished after death? Different cultures and religions deal with these questions in many ways.

For the Chinese, there is continuity between life and death. The spirits of the dead can affect the living. Ancestors must be properly attended to and revered by their descendents. Dutiful relatives will be rewarded in this world with good health and prosperity; those who are neglectful invite calamity. Ghosts of the uncared-for dead, called "wild ghosts," wander in the nether region and can cause trouble to punish the living. They include those who have no descendants or who died far from their families as well as those who have done evil deeds during their lifetime. It cannot be overemphasized how much reverent treatment of the dead impacts the consciousness of the living Chinese. The dead cannot be abandoned or forgotten.

The rituals involved with Chinese funerals and burials aim at providing for the comfort of the deceased so that the person may have ease in the afterlife. The deceased is given offerings of food, clothing, material goods (represented by paper effigies) and symbolic money—all the needed amenities for a life of comfort. Food is left at the grave and paper representations of worldly possessions are burned at the cemetery to convey the objects into the spirit realm.

This concern for the departed continues annually at the Clear Brightness Festival or *Chingming* (Qingming) every April, the fourth month of the lunar calendar, and another observance in autumn, *Chung Yeung* (Chong Yang, also often called *Chong Jiu* meaning "double nine") occurring on ninth day of the ninth month of the lunar calendar. On these special days, relatives or friends sweep the graves and propitiate the deceased with food and other offerings. The neglected dead are also called "hungry ghosts," because there is no one to "feed" or worship them. There is even a separate feast day for them on the fifteenth day of the seventh lunar month called the Hungry Ghosts Festival or *Yu Lan* (Gui) in which wandering ghosts are released from the underworld and appeased with offerings in public places. Chinese immigrants would have followed these traditions to care for the graves of the dead. Relatives living near by, fellow clan members, or friends from the same village would not have neglected their deceased compatriots.

Since most of the Chinese people immigrating to California were separated from their families in China, it was necessary for their countrymen or district association members to oversee the funeral, care for the cemetery, and assure that the bones of the dead would be transported back to China where they could be reburied and lovingly cared for by family members.

Chinese funerals in America could be noisy occasions where musicians accompanied the funeral procession playing loud cacophonous music on gongs and drums along with the explosions of firecrackers, all to frighten away evil spirits. Off-white paper perforated with holes, "spirit money," was scattered along the street to confuse or bribe evil spirits from finding the burial location. A Chinese funeral in Sacramento was described in the newspaper:

> A Chinese funeral took place yesterday, the deceased being Ah Cheow, the proprietor of a Chinese boarding house on I street. Before the funeral took place a first class Chinese lunch, designed only, however, for hungry spirits, was spread upon a table in front of the house. A roasted pig formed a prominent feature of the lay out, accompanied by roast chicken and accompaniments. The remains of the deceased were conveyed to the cemetery by a hearse, followed by a wagon containing the fare above described and several Chinese women, who, in the capacity of chief mourners, distributed along the streets through which they passed slips of marked paper, the significance of which we are not enlightened upon.[3]

In cities like San Francisco and Sacramento funerals for wealthy or prominent members of the Chinese community (usually merchants) were elaborate affairs consisting of processions with people carrying decorative paper banners, flags and paper lanterns; a coffin borne on a wagon; horses and wagons laden with food, flowers, incense, paper offerings and personal effects; as well as hired mourners wailing in grief around the wooden coffin as described above. Traditionally, the processions would circle three rounds in Chinatown for the deceased to say goodbye to the community and friends. Most likely, funerals were more modest in Amador County, where Chinese merchants were probably not as conspicuously wealthy.

The Chinese in Amador County had separate graveyards from whites, perhaps by choice since bones of the dead were periodically exhumed.

---

3 *Sacramento Daily Union*, April 4, 1863.

110

Jackson had at least three identified Chinese cemeteries: in Jackson Gate, in central Jackson (now covered by the Jackson city maintenance yard) close to the Protestant cemetery, and in south Jackson west edge of Gordon Hill by South Street.[4] The deceased of Ione, Drytown and Volcano were buried in Chinese cemeteries close to those Chinatowns. Their remains are long gone, transported back to China for burial in their home villages. Fiddletown's Chinese cemetery gives the greatest insight into the practices, dedication, and support within the Chinese community for their departed brethren, because in Fiddletown important records have been found and translated.

---

4 Cenotto, *Logan's Alley*, vol. 2, pg 165 and *Amador County Historic Resources Inventory*, "Chinese Cemetery Site, Jackson" and "Jackson Gate Chinese Cemetery".

FIDDLETOWN'S CHINESE CEMETERY:
PORTRAIT OF A COMMUNITY

THE CHINESE CEMETERY IN FIDDLETOWN

Fiddletown's Chinese cemetery was located off of west Main Street about a quarter mile to the south on Quartz Mountain Road, the old entry to Fiddletown from Drytown. The sites of Chinese cemeteries in California and elsewhere often conformed to the principle of *feng shui* or geomancy, widely applied in China for choosing the most auspicious location. The natural setting, especially hills, trees and water, was used for locating burial places. It was desirable to have hills or mountains in the back, protecting the bodies from winds.[1]

The Fiddletown cemetery was located in a sylvan setting on a knoll facing east, near a larger hill. According to a Fiddletown resident who visited the exhumed graves as a child, deceased were buried along the slope of the hill. No traces remain now of the cemetery. The remains were exhumed long ago and the area is currently owned by Amador County and used as a septic leach field.

The cemetery was extremely important to Fiddletown's Chinese community. Three books, written in Chinese and discovered in the Chew Kee Store, attest to its prominence: Fiddletown's *Cemetery Record Book*, *Donation Records for Restoration of our Cemetery,* and the *Record Book of the Deceased*. These books give a portrait of the community, living and deceased and will be discussed in separate chapters.

THE CEMETERY RECORD BOOK

The history of the Fiddletown Chinese cemetery is documented in a cemetery record book, labeled *Mei Sun*, that tracked the donations, repairs, and expenses for the cemetery from 1870-1904.[2] This book reveals the origins of donors, the contribution of women and relationships with other communities. It also shows that Fiddletown's Chinese community was

1 Rouse, Wendy L, "A History of Chinese Death Rituals" in *Chinese American Death Rituals* by Sue Fawn Chung and Priscilla Wegars.

2 The *Cemetery Record Book* was translated by Dr. Sonia Ng, who also discovered the use of *Mei Sun* in another source. *Mei Sun* was used as a generic term for "cemetery" in reference to the Lone Mountain Cemetery in San Francisco where Chinese immigrants were buried.

more active towards the turn of the nineteenth century and beginning of the twentieth than implied by U.S. Census counts.

In 1870 the Fiddletown Chinese community held a major fund drive to raise money to build the cemetery. Income and expenses were carefully itemized in the Cemetery Record Book. Land for the cemetery was purchased for $60 (about $1,100 in 2013 values). Carpenters, stone masons and other construction workers were paid for labor costs during construction. Even expenses for wooden planks and nails were accounted for. Although no evidence of a structure remains, it can be deduced that a shrine with an altar for candles and offerings was constructed, especially since expenses for candles were itemized each year. The shrine may have been built of marble, which was available from a quarry between Fiddletown and Plymouth. The shrine would have included a "burner," usually made of brick or masonry, for igniting the symbolic offerings. Markers (stone tablets or headstones) made of stone, wood, or marble contained the identification of the deceased at gravesites, including their district in China and date and time of death.

The list of donors in 1870 gives an insight into the composition and comparative wealth of the Chinese community. During this period, donors included their district of origin in China, another example of immigrants identifying with their home district. The largest number of donors was from the three counties of Sam Yup: 90 people from the county of Punyu, 69 from the county of Shunduk, and 10 from the county of Namhoi gave money. They contributed a total of $215 (about $4,000). Other donors were from the counties of Toishan (43), and Heungshan (17) now known as Chungshan.

Of particular interest, thirty-three women donors are singled out and listed on separate pages. Sing Choy (Foo Kee's companion) and Sigh Choy (wife of Chew Kee) were among the contributors, as well as many women who were prostitutes. While the amount that the women gave was not great, the fact that they had disposable income and chose to contribute to the cemetery was significant. The women were participating members of the community, including those who were prostitutes.

All together, 229 people donated $318 in 1870 (equivalent to $5,700)[3] to create the cemetery, contributions that involved the entire Chinese community, no matter what county they came from in China. Funds left over from construction were distributed for safe-keeping between two

---

3   Currency value equivalents in 2013 are based on conversion data from Oregon State University.

stores, the Foo Kee General Store and the Lee Kee Store, and two trusted individuals, Leung Yiu Tai and Yeung Choy Gwong. When money was needed to pay for expenses such as candles and property tax, withdrawals were meticulously recorded. All monies collected and distributed were accounted for in the Cemetery Record Book. This documentation provides more evidence of how capable Chinese immigrants were in the area of finance.

More campaigns to raise money for cemetery repairs and supplies occurred in 1879, 1880, 1891 and 1903. Reflecting the declining population of Chinese throughout the years, each fund drive had fewer donors and less money was raised. Donors were no longer identified by their county of origin in China. Perhaps birthplace became less important as immigrants remained longer in towns. Starting in 1890, contributions to the cemetery came from other communities including Jackson and unnamed small towns, in addition to donations from Fiddletown. This shows that the Fiddletown Chinese community was in contact with Chinese from other local Chinatowns. As these towns became less populated with Chinese residents, Fiddletown's Chinese cemetery increased in use and importance.

CHINESE CREDIT UNION

The Cemetery Record Book tracked another important function. Collectively, the Fiddletown Chinese community operated their own bank or credit union in an informal group called a *wui* (hui), following similar practices existing in southern China. The transactions were documented in this book as part of the cemetery operation. Participants, including the Chinese women of Fiddletown, knew and trusted each other with a collective pooling of community funds. Each person contributed money, and deposited it in merchants' stores. Loans were made to individual men and women as needed and would be awarded to the person bidding to pay the highest interest. From 1883 to 1886, the *wui* had an income of $230 (equivalent to about $5,350) in addition to $14 generated in interest.

Fiddletown's merchants played an important role as the major custodians and lenders of the funds collected. In the 1870s and early 1880s, Foo Kee was a key figure in keeping deposits and disbursing the loans from his store. Chew Kee and his store took over from the mid-1880s through first decade of the twentieth century. Small funds were also deposited in the Wo Sing Store in the late 1890s and early twentieth century. The merchants obviously had stature and a high level of trust from Fiddletown's Chinese residents.

The Cemetery Record Book is a rare find that documents the workings of Fiddletown's Chinese community. Members of the community, including women, helped each other financially, not only coming together to support and maintain the cemetery but also by collectively raising money that could then be lent out to individuals in need of capital. In this way, the Chinese community could be economically self-sustaining.

Figure 36. Chinese cemetery location. *E. Zorbas*

THE CHEW KEE STORE

CHEW KEE, MERCHANT AND GAMBLER

The merchant Chew Kee (Chao Ji) is important to Fiddletown's history, not only for the many objects, books, and documents that he left behind in the store that bears his name, but also for his influence on the Chinese community. He was a gambler and a businessman, whose generosity may have contributed to his financial difficulties.

Chew Kee hailed from Punyu County in the Sam Yup district, home of many merchants. In 1857 he immigrated to California at the age of twenty. Although later was known by his store name of Chew Kee (*Kee* meaning store), his last name was *Ngan* and his first name was Chew (Yen Chao Ji). He also had other names, in common Chinese practice: *Gun Chew* and a respectful form of address, *Bak Hung*.

Ngan Chew appears as a donor for the Fiddletown cemetery in 1879, but he rose to prominence in the mid-1880s. At the beginning of that decade, he was forty-three years old and his wife, Sigh Choy (Sai Choy), meaning "the younger Choy," was thirty-four. She had arrived in California in 1863 when she was only seventeen years old. Nine years later, in 1872 they married. This information about them was recorded in the 1900 Census. An earlier census in 1870 lists a woman named Sigh Choy of the same age "keeping house" with two other women. These women may have been prostitutes. It was not unusual for Chinese prostitutes to marry Chinese men, since there was a paucity of Chinese women in California.

GAMBLING

The life of Ngan Chew (hereafter referred to as Chew Kee) and Sigh Choy before their occupancy of the herb store is not known. An examination of the 1880 Census lists a couple whose ages match theirs— *Ah Chu*, who managed a gambling house, and *Sarah*, his wife. The gambling house across the way was owned by Yee Fung; much coming and going took place between the herb store and the gambling house. It is plausible that Yee Fung Cheung, busy with his other enterprises in Sacramento and Virginia City, turned over the operation of the gambling house and his store to Chew Kee.

Furthermore, Chew was one of five shareholders of the gambling establishment. The Fiddletown gambling house, called *Fook Tai Chong* or *Fortune Peaceful Gambling House*, was begun on "an auspicious day in 1884."[1] Its shareholders together raised $700, the equivalent of almost $16,000 in 2013 values. Chew and two others bought shares worth $100 (equivalent 2013 value of $2,300). Fung Fong and Cheung How Cheung held shares worth $200 each. A ledger found in the Chew Kee Store tracked the daytime and evening income of the gambling house during its first year of operation. It is quite evident that Chew Kee ran the gambling house.

At the Chew Kee Store, customers were able to purchase whatever paraphernalia they needed for gambling. A book sold in the store gave tips embedded in the Chinese classic, *Story of Three Kingdoms*, for a gambling game of thirty six characters called *Zi Fa*. Playing cards, mah jong tiles, fortune telling cards, and dominoes (*pai gow*) were all available in the store.

Everything that was needed to buy and track sales of pigeon tickets for the eighty character lottery game, *Bak Gup Pil*, was right there. The Chew Kee Store contained carved wooden stamps (chops), each representing a different Chinese character used to make up the pigeon ticket. Other stamps were used for bookkeeping and to record the number of sales made by various agents and distributors.[2] It is probable that Chinese residents from other Amador County towns bought pigeon tickets and, like those in Fiddletown, eagerly awaited news of the lottery drawings at Fortune Peaceful Gambling House.

MERCHANT AND MERCHANDISE

When Chew Kee took over the herb store in 1884, he changed it into a general merchandise and grocery store that also provided medicine. Under his management, the original herb drawers, altar, baskets, prescription packets and other items from Dr. Yee Fung Cheung remained in the commercial front part of the store. Herbal and other medicines continued to be dispensed to treat illnesses. These included preparations imported from China, American patent medicines, and concoctions in reused American bottles and vials. There were medicines to treat malaria, headaches, bruised muscles, eye trouble, diarrhea, animal infections transmitted to humans, etc. "Ground crane bone" otherwise known as

1 The book listing the name and shareholders of the gambling house was translated in 2013 by Dr. Sonia Ng. "Chong" is a term used to denote a gambling house or a company that could potentially operate several gambling houses.
2 Russell, "Chew Kee Store," pg. 39-40.

"cut powder" was used as a treatment for stab wounds; "ash of tobacco" was recommended for "fallen injuries" or bruises. Opium was available for purchase, as well as tear-out slips in Chinese with prescriptions on how to stop smoking opium.

Like many businessmen, Chew Kee hoped that his enterprise would be successful. On cabinet drawers behind the front counter, he added good luck signs for his business, visible to customers. Written in large Chinese characters on red paper, they remain in the store. Translated into English they urge: *Keep working hard, going to win*; *open up future, big fortune*; and *river never stops, keep customers coming*. Chew Kee placed orders for foodstuff and goods with Chinese stores in Stockton and San Francisco. He expanded the inventory of his store to include such merchandise as cigars, tobacco, beer, Chinese wine, whiskey, dried meat and fish, vegetables, tea, opium and opium pipes. The store's stock encompassed firecrackers, mirrors, ink and writing utensils, combs and books. Rice, pearl barley and tapioca were stored in brown stoneware jars imported from China.

The merchant Chew Kee was literate—a rarity for many Chinese immigrants, most of whom were illiterate peasants. In his store, customers could receive correspondence from family in China and also

Figure 37. Office in Chew Kee Store. *D. Zorbas*

119

obtain assistance in drafting responses. Slotted metal holders for holding envelopes are still in the store. Frequently there were scribes at both ends of the letter writing. Many books in Chinese were found in the store, including fortune telling books, a face-reading book, medical remedies for various ailments, a pharmacopeia, a volume with advice on avoiding bad behavior that could lead to Hell, and a book with sample business letters. Chew sold yearly almanacs having sections on astrology, dream interpretation, Confucian wisdom, numerology, etc. The annual calendar helped customers determine auspicious days and times for various endeavors, such as opening a business or conducting a wedding.

Chew kept up with events in China and in the U.S., subscribing to many Chinese language newspapers from San Francisco, including *The Chinese Free Press*, *Chinese World*, and *The Weekly Occidental*. China was in turmoil at the end of the nineteenth century, poised between reform efforts, conservative opposition, and the emergence of nationalism. In 1900 the anti-Western Boxer Rebellion with attacks on foreigners and Christian missionaries, gained support from the Qing Dynasty, only to be quelled by an invasion of 20,000 foreign troops representing eight nations, an overall disaster for China. A Chinese-language newspaper reporting on these clashes remains posted in the Chew Kee Store.

This store also functioned as the gathering place for the Chinese residents of Fiddletown. Chinese visitors to the store, lonely for their home country, could come to discuss events taking place across the Pacific Ocean. Here people could reminisce about life and family back home in China, relax, smoke opium, talk about gambling wins and losses, and share meals.

FAMILY

When Chew Kee was about forty-nine and Sigh Choy forty, they were requested to take custody of a very young boy. His parents, who also lived in Fiddletown, were returning to their home in China and could not take the child with them. It is likely that the boy's parents and Chew were from the same village in China in Punyu County. If not relatives, they were certainly close friends who could be trusted to care for a precious son. They referred to Sigh Choy as a "godmother." Chew and Sigh Choy, being childless, would have welcomed the opportunity to raise the boy, Fong Chow Yow. They added a small child's cot next to their plank bed in

Figure 38. Bedroom with child's bed. *D.Zorbas*

the bedroom. Chow Yow became their "adopted son," whom they reared as their own and later formally adopted.

Since Chew was married and now had a son, a new addition built of wood in the 1890s was located beyond the iron door where the shop ended. Here a room for cooking and washing was appended to the thick rear adobe walls. The walls, floors, trough for washing, and shelves for storing dishware and utensils were all hand hewn, made from wooden boards and boxes.

As the boy grew, space for the family was expanded in another adjoining wooden addition with a second kitchen, a living space, and a second bedroom where Chow Yow could sleep. Doors led to two outside sheds. With these changes, Sigh Choy obtained a cast-iron stove for the first kitchen and a built-in wok for the second kitchen where she could prepare traditional Chinese food, essential for health, sustenance and fellowship. She also cooked in the outdoor shed that contained a very large wok oven where food could be prepared for a large group. This is another indication that the store was a community gathering place.

FINANCIAL TROUBLES

Chew Kee took over Foo Kee's role of leadership in the Chinese community. He was entrusted with community savings and helped raise contributions for various charities in his store. He was also a frequent donor. As a merchant, he was addressed by fellow Chinese in correspondence as *Great Bo Ho*, a respectful way to refer to a business.

The start of Chew Kee's financial difficulties began when he assumed custody of the properties that had belonged to the merchant Foo Kee. In 1887 he obtained a $200 loan for the three Foo Kee properties from Frank Uhlinger, a local farmer.

Two and one-half years later, he borrowed $400 from the Fiddletown merchant Lee Kee and his partner, Ah Sing. This time, the loan encompassed additional properties—the Foo Kee properties, the "Dobe house with sheds attached facing Main Street and known as the Chew Kee Store," and one-third of a nearby lot and building formerly owned by the herb doctor, E. [Yee] Fung and purchased from Ah Gin. The loan was due in six months, with interest of 1 percent each month. A document requested by Chew Kee in 1893 verified that this loan was paid off.

The mortgage for all of the properties above was now held by German born farmer George Barge, who lent Chew $200 in March of 1894. The document noted that the Chew Kee Store was part of a larger parcel formerly owned by E.C. Simpson. (In actuality the store never had separate title, which was not discovered until many years later).

The financial situation continued to worsen. Chew Kee was a generous man, perhaps too generous. Many IOU's were found in the store, such as one for seven boxes of cigarettes with a note, "straighten

Figure 39. Wok kitchen addition. *D. Zorbas*

bill another time." Forms written in Chinese for customers, translated as *"Thanks for visiting and picking up the unpaid merchandise,"* indicated that goods were sold on credit. Chew Kee may have been too lenient with his customers, another reason that he became saddled with debt. His financial situation deteriorated to the point that Ratto's Law Collection Agency in San Francisco sent an undated letter in the 1890s written in Chinese:[3]

> I wish to inform you that we sent you a letter the day before yesterday
> to collect the $120.00 owed but we have not heard anything from you
> yet. Is there any reason? We are writing to you again and please make
> payment immediately upon receipt this letter. If there is any further
> delay, we will ask that the notary public to seal off your property. Full
> payment must be made. Do not say that we have not made any advanced
> notice. Please make sure you respond by the 28th this month. Any delay
> will cause you disadvantage.

Desperate perhaps, Chew Kee sold his business on December 23, 1896 for $200 in gold coin to the business of Man Lung & Co. His entire inventory was conveyed to Man Lung, described as "the whole of goods, wares, and merchandise and fixtures without reservation now contained

Figure 40. Chew Kee certificate of residence. *Amador County Archives*

3 Translated by Kai Lui, San Francisco, November 2005.

in my store and mercantile business together with the good will thereof. Also one horse and harness and one cart."

The mortgage held by George Barge for the properties was still outstanding. Chew Kee was unable to meet the obligations of the loan and the properties were sold on public auction in 1898. On August 6, Barge purchased the various parcels for $390, gaining possession in February 1899. Four years later, he sold the Foo Kee properties on the south side of Main Street to Postmaster William "Billie" Brown, owner of the blacksmith forge and house nearby.

INTO THE TWENTIETH CENTURY

Nonetheless, Chew Kee continued to live and operate his business in the same store into the early twentieth century, perhaps working with Man Lung Company. He ordered food and other merchandise from merchants in

Figure 41. Business with San Francisco store. *Chew Kee Store*

Sacramento and San Francisco,[4] maintaining his contacts in these cities.

In 1900, Chew received a letter from his brother in China, Ngan Chow Sing (Ngan Bing Sun) asking him to return to China and if not, to send money. Chow Sing wrote, "My dear younger brother, you have gone overseas for forty-four years; not only did you rarely send money home but you even rarely sent letters home. Is it because you enjoy life so happily there that you have forgotten about our parents' tombs here in this poor town?"[5] The brothers had been separated for more than a generation; Chew Kee had settled in California's Fiddletown with no intention to return to China. Even with debt, he fared better in Gold Mountain.

Meanwhile, China was undergoing great change. The Qing Dynasty, which had controlled China since 1644, was severely weakened, its belated reforms unable to deflect growing revolutionary movements. By

4 Envelopes and some grocery orders show dealings with the stores Hoy Kee & Co. and Wo Own Yu Kee in Sacramento and Yee Chong & Co., Oy Wo Tong & Co. and Yee Shan in San Francisco.
5 Translated by Dr. Sonia Ng from the *Chew Kee Store Miscellany* collection at the Ethnic Studies Library, University of California, Berkeley.

December 1911, reformers took control of the south and west of China, which broke off from the rest of the empire. To spread the news of this great event, a 1911 Chinese language newspaper hailing the Chinese Revolution was posted by Chew Kee at the entry to the store. On February 12, 1912, the empire fell to a new republic headed by Dr. Sun Yatsen (Sun Zhongshan), who had rallied support in California among Chinese for years.

Chew Kee continued in business through 1912. As other merchants departed from Fiddletown or died, he became caretaker of their properties including the Wo Sing store across the street and property two parcels east of his store, which had once been owned by Yee Fung. Chew's wife, Sigh Choy, had died several years before. When he was seventy-six years old in 1913, he deeded these properties along with the Chew Kee Store and gambling house, with "love and affection" to his adopted son, Fong Chow Yow. Chew Kee died one month later on July 18, 1913 and was buried in Fiddletown's Chinese cemetery.

FROM FONG CHOW YOW TO JIMMIE CHOW

The child *Fong Chow Yow* (Feng Qiu You), raised and adopted by Chew Kee and Sigh Choy, was born in Fiddletown on October 27, 1885, one year after the Chinatown was destroyed by an arson fire. His given name of *Chow Yow*, reflecting the season of his birth, meant "*autumn possession*." His last name was transliterated as *Fong*, but pronounced in Cantonese as *Fung*.

Chow Yow's birth parents were residents of Fiddletown. His father, Fung Fong (Fong Huang)[1] was one of the five shareholders of the Fortune Peaceful Gambling House and a donor to the Chinese cemetery.

Figure 42. Fong Chow Yow with queue. *Amador County Archives*

---

1 After reading the father's name in letters in letters and in documents, Dr. Sonia Ng concluded that character for Fong was used incorrectly as a surname in written Chinese. The actual surname is Fung, written with a different Chinese character. Fong was the father's first name.

Figure 43. Chow Yow Certificate of Residence. *Chew Kee Store*

Several long-time Fiddletown residents swore in a 1902 document[2] that they knew both of his parents, who "left the United States some time not long after the boy was born, leaving the said boy in charge of a Chinese merchant by name of Chew Kee who raised him." As Chow Yow later found out, his birth father returned to China first, abandoning the idea of getting rich in Gold Mountain. Afterwards, his mother departed for China, leaving behind her first-born and eldest son with a godmother, Sigh Choy.

The Fung family returned to their home in the village of *Zhu Liao* (Jook Liu Tsuen), Punyu County, in the Sam Yup district where Chew Kee also came from. One can only speculate why they left behind a young son. Much later in his life, Chow Yow claimed that he was too sickly as a child to make the journey to China. However, since the boy was born in the U.S., his legitimacy to permanently reside there was assured at a time when most Chinese were excluded from entering the country. A son residing in the United States would have better prospects of employment and thereby be in a position to help provide for his family back in China.

2 This document was probably required for Chow Yow's formal adoption by Chew Kee. It was signed by residents Christopher Schallhorn, J.H. Campbell, H. Bradigan, E.R. Yates and John Votaw

The Geary Act of 1892 required Chinese to obtain a certificate to prove legal residency, something no other group was required to do. Chew Kee complied with the extended final deadline for registration. In May 1884, he obtained Certificates of Residence for himself (under the name Chow Kee) and for his adopted son. He was identified as a merchant, a preferred status since the enactment and extension of the Chinese Exclusion Act. Fong Chow Yow, then age eight years old (one year discrepancy with his 1885 birth date) was identified as "son of merchant" and "native born son of person other than laborer."

GROWING UP IN FIDDLETOWN

Chow Yow grew up immersed in Chinese culture, nurtured by his adoptive parents. In the Chew Kee Store and home, Chow was surrounded by the implements of Chinese life, from the herb doctor's paraphernalia to Chew Kee's merchandise. Chinese New Year was celebrated every year with new banners and special food, offerings were made at the family altar to deities and ancestors, and most of the store's customers were Chinese. Cantonese was the language spoken at home. His adopted father taught Chow Yow to read enough Chinese to help out at the store, no small accomplishment because of the difficulty of written Chinese. As he grew up, the boy most likely assisted Chew Kee with ordering, stocking and selling merchandise.

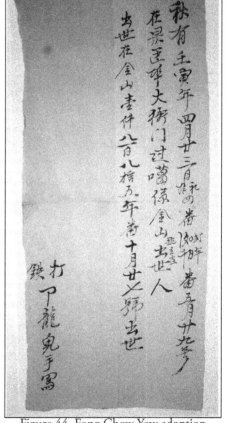

Figure 44. Fong Chow Yow adoption certificate, 1902. *Amador County Archives*

Chow reminisced about the town in his only interview, conducted when he was seventy- two years

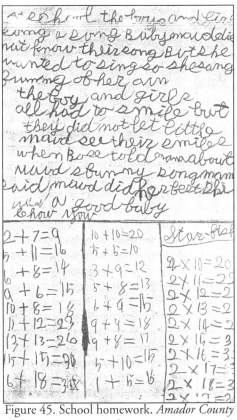

Figure 45. School homework. *Amador County Archives*

old. "I can remember when I was a little boy. There was a gambling house across the street. Upstairs were sing-song girls. You could hear Chinese music all over Chinatown. Plenty of excitement here then. There were thousands of Chinese here….Chinese riders from the gambling den would jump on their horses and carry their lottery tickets all the way to Plymouth and Drytown without stopping. Fiddletown had the most of all."[3] There were not nearly as many Chinese as described by Chow, but he obviously felt encompassed by the Chinese community. The "sing-song girls" mentioned in the Fortune Peaceful Gambling House were most likely prostitutes, who also entertained customers with music.

At the time, Fiddletown (Oleta) was a village of only three hundred people. Its commerce centered in the English speaking part of town, just to the east of Chinatown along Main Street. Chinese residents also patronized stores in that section and several people, including Chew Kee and Sigh Choy, did speak some English.

The boy Chow Yow had to adapt to the ways of the entire town and the local roughneck culture. Like other children in town, Chow attended Fiddletown's one-room schoolhouse (then called Oleta School) where he learned how to read and write English. He was especially good in math. It was probably there that he got the American nickname *Jimmie*. He wore his hair in the style denoting obedience to the Qing Dynasty in

---

3 Yee, Johnny. "Anecdotes of Chinatown" *in 1978 Souvenir Book, Los Angeles Chinatown.* (Los Angeles, Chinese Chamber of Commerce).

China, head shaved in front and remaining hair plaited in a long braid called a queue. This plus his Asian features made him stand out as the only Chinese in school. Initially bullied by the local boys, he fought back with his fists and earned their respect, acquiring the nickname "Jimmie Corbett Chow" after a famous heavy-weight boxer of the era. He may have been small, but he was feisty.

Chow was still attending school at age thirteen, but like many children in town, his education ended early (at the most, he completed eighth grade) because of economic necessity and lack of transportation to the high school in Sutter Creek. Meanwhile, he had developed friendships with other boys in town, accompanying them on fishing and hunting excursions in the nearby Sierra Nevada, where there was abundant wildlife. He also formed a life-long friendship with Yee, daughter of a local Chinese grocer. A few years older than Chow Yow, she was also raised in Fiddletown.

When Chow was seventeen years old, he was formally adopted by Chew Kee. The legal document cannot be obtained because of privacy restrictions, but the Chinese version was found in the Chew Kee Store, hand written with ink and brush by Wai Lung Yee (Wei Long Er), an herbal doctor who specialized in injuries. It states that Chow Yow, on May 29, 1902, "Thursday in Western Calendar, was adopted at the Grand Government Office in Jackson. He was born in Fiddletown [on] Gold Mountain on October 17, 1885 in the Western Calendar."

LETTERS FROM FAMILY IN CHINA

Figure 46. Family letter from Canton, 1908. *Ethnic Studies Library*

Chow Yow began to receive letters from his family in China when he was around twenty years old. Was this a surprise or did Chew Kee and Sigh Choy keep him informed about his natural parents? Did he welcome the communication from China? Did Chew Kee help him to read and understand the various Chinese characters in the letter?

The letters arrived through intermediaries, a complicated journey since Chinese lettering was unintelligible to Americans. They originated from the family's village, Zhu Liao (Jook Liu Tsuen), in Guangdong Province. Chow Yow's father, Fung Fong, was a farmer. Since most Chinese peasants were illiterate, the letters were most likely written by a scribe in Guangzhou (Canton City) and hand carried to Hong Kong (Xianggang) where they were sent by ship to San Francisco. From there, they were relayed through a network of stores and personal contacts until they reached their destination. The envelopes were usually addressed with the store name written in English as well as in Chinese. In the Fongs' case, several letters were sent to Jow Moke, c/o George West & Sons in Stockton. Mrs. Jow Moke was Chow Yow's childhood friend Yee from Fiddletown. The families were connected in some way, perhaps from the same or nearby villages in Punyu County. Chow Yow and Yee corresponded in English for many years.

In the first letter received from his father, Fung Fong wrote that he had heard from a villager (Fung Chiu) that Chow Yow was over twenty years old. After briefly explaining to his son about returning to China from Gold Mountain he implored, "Here I purposely write to ask you, Chow Yow that you must come back to your hometown in China and not stay in the foreign county. Therefore, I asked Yeung Sing to see you and urge you to come home to China. By the way, you also have a younger brother named Bun Yiu."[4] It is interesting to note that the father's informant or intermediary was not Chew Kee. Chow's adopted father had raised and grown fond of him, and perhaps at heart did not want his adopted son to be reunited with his birth family.

Chow Yow's brother, Bun Yiu (Bin Yao) wrote to him in 1906, about the same time as his father did, describing the family in China. Chow learned that he had four siblings counting Bun Yiu —an older sister who

---

4 Originals and microfilm copies of letters from Fong Chow Yow's family as well as other documents from the Chew Kee Store are contained in the *Chew Kee Store Miscellany* collection held by the Ethnic Studies Library, University of California, Berkeley. Letters from microfilm copies have been translated by Philip Choy and Yuet Ho Tsui in 2008 and 2009, and reviewed and expanded by Dr. Sonia Ng in 2014.

was forty years old, a younger brother about twenty-two years old[5] and a younger sister, eighteen years old. At this time, his father was seventy-six years old and his mother was forty-four. With the proximity of age between the older sister and mother, it is clear Fung Fong had married a second younger wife in California. He was around fifty-five and this wife was twenty-two when Chow Yow was born. Nothing more is known about Fung Fong's first wife or his second wife, Chow's mother.

Now that Chow Yow had reached maturity, the family continuously pressed him to send money and "return home." Chow Yow, as a first-born son, bore the filial duty to respect and honor his parents, a duty deeply ingrained in Chinese culture. It was expected that he would help support the family. His father Fung Fong wrote with the voice of authority and urged Chow Yow to find a wife in China. Marriage would continue the family line and hopefully result in the birth of sons. His brother was getting married and if Chow did not come home to marry, money sent would be set aside instead for Bun Yiu's wedding.

Chow worked hard to save money for the family, who no doubt believed that everyone in America was rich. In the 1910 Census, he was listed as a farm laborer and his earnings were meager. For a couple of years he had lived in a house on Main Street, where property had been divided up among a few Chinese residents. Afterwards he lived independently elsewhere in Fiddletown, most likely close to the farm where he worked. His adopted mother, Sigh Choy, had died a few years before and Chew Kee at age seventy-three was living alone in the store as a widower.

Receipts and correspondence found in the Chew Kee Store demonstrate that Chow was a dutiful son who regularly sent money "home" to China. The money, sent as gold coin, was relayed through Yeung Sing and other intermediaries. In 1906 and 1907, he sent "protection" money via a pro-Imperialist organization in Stockton to his parent's village. This was during a period when there were revolts in China against the Qing Dynasty. Chinese organizations in the U.S. kept up with and even tried to influence political movements in China, in this case supporting the imperial regime. Three receipts for Chow's donation to this cause were found in the Chew Kee Store.

---

5 The younger brother would have been Bun Yiu. Age is calculated differently in China; a newborn is considered to be one years old, gaining a second year on Chinese New Year. This is known as nominal age in contrast with actual age. The two brothers were very close in age implying that they may have had different mothers since Fung Fong had two wives.

Bun Yiu sent an undated letter from Guangzhou via Sun Tung Wo (Xin Tong He) merchandise store in San Francisco to the Chew Kee Store. The economic plight of the family had worsened.

On February 4th, I received a one dollar gold coin, weigh 2.2 taels[6] from outside the country. I received the gold with a letter and cashed in without problems. Father and brother have worked hard at farming without other means of living. Father is getting old and no longer goes out looking for job; the financial situation is even worse than ever to maintain the household expenses. Please consider to return home once you have reached the saving goal and do not stay abroad any longer than you have to. If you don't have plans to return home in the near future, please remember it is necessary to continue to send money home for the financial needs.[7]

Through the years, Chow received several similar letters (always written in Chinese), from Bun Yiu, from his sister and from his father. In 1908 Fung Fong acknowledged the receipt of another one dollar gold coin, brought by intermediary Yeong Sing. "It is received but I think it is difficult for you to make money overseas. You have to take care of your own health and the right thing to do is to come home earlier. This is the wish of mine as your father...I think you have grown old and it is important for you to come home soon to get married. If you do not come back, you have to send money. Members of the family are all well and you don't have to worry."[8]

In about 1912 Chow's brother Bun Yiu joined the Chinese Revolution, enlisting in the army as his patriotic duty despite the poor pay. Money was still needed to support the family. Two years after the Revolution, Chow hosted Wong Bok Yue, one of the founders of the San Francisco newspaper *Young China*, who was visiting Fiddletown to gather funds for reform in China. His presence indicated that the town and surroundings still had a supportive Chinese community sympathetic to the republican ideals of the Revolution.

Chow received a short note in English from a friend, Bing Su Yut Ming, mailed from San Francisco on April 17, 1914. His friend wrote that he was taking the steamer the following day to China and he, too, urged

---

6   http://en.wikipedia.org/wiki/Tael. One silver Canton tael weighed 37.5 grams or 1.2 oz.

7   Letter from Chew Kee Store translated by Vicki Beaton and Chung Kong, August 2003.

8   Excerpt from letter on microfilm at the Ethnic Studies Library, University of California, Berkeley translated by Dr. Sonia Ng.

Figure 47. Hong Kong photo, probably Bun Yiu. *Amador County Archives*

Chow to "return to China as soon as you can." Several months later, he received a desperate letter from his brother imploring him to send more money. This letter was sent from Hong Kong on November 16, 1914[9].

> The trace of the geese is far separated from us. I think of you so dearly and it is hard to set aside the feeling. I believe that you are healthy and doing well as time goes by and this is my best wish from far away. Life is hard in China which you can tell. I work as a laborer to make a living but since this is a not a permanent job, sometimes there may be no work, which can make the situation worse. My son was born on May 27, which adds more expenses to the family. Further than that, I have been staying home for several months since there is no work and life has become

9 This letter from Chew Kee Store was translated by Kai Lui, July 28, 2006, later reviewed and partially re-translated by Dr. Sonia Ng, March 2014. Dr. Ng explained, "Trace of the geese" is the metaphor for far separation between lovers, close friends, or family members. In Chinese literature for over two thousand years it was said that the geese carried letters or messages from far away." Chinese use many metaphors, including another one in the letter, "fish trapped in a dry rut" which conveys the sense of helpless despair.

harder.

As it is the custom in our village that whenever a boy is born, we need to follow the "lantern lighting" practice which will need several tens of dollars.[10] Since I do not have work now and the date is approaching soon, it will be difficult for me to raise this sum of money. And, given the indifferent feeling of fellow villagers, it will not be easy to borrow money from them. I have no way but, shamefacedly, to ask that you, in consideration of a brother's difficulty, send some money home as soon as possible so as to relieve the fish trapped in dry rut. I appreciate your help very much.

The letter ended with the usual plea for Chow to return home and if not, to send money through remittance or by way of a Chinese friend.

A search of immigration and passenger ship records at the National Archives[11] did not turn up evidence that Chow visited his family in China; furthermore, he stated in his sole interview that he never went to China. Although the plight of his family must have affected him deeply, making the trip would be an expense that he could ill afford. Expectations from his family were high, and he was better off sending money from his earnings in Fiddletown than struggling to make a living in China. It was clear from family letters that life there was even harder.

BECOMING JIMMIE CHOW

By now he was living as Jimmie Chow. He was thirty years old and had grown into a sturdy and strong man, capable of hard work. He had not gone to China to find a bride, as urged by his father. There were few unmarried Chinese women in California and like many Chinese men in the U.S. he remained a bachelor for his entire life. What Jimmie Chow lacked in female companionship, he found in friendship. He had many good friends in Fiddletown and was welcomed into their homes. One of

10 As explained in the Hong Kong Museum of History, "Around the 12th day of the first Chinese lunar month, a 'lighting lantern' ceremony is held in Hong Kong's clan-based villages to initiate male children born into the village in the past year as new clan members. The newly initiated village sons are announced to the gods by the hanging of paper lanterns in the ancestral hall and, sometimes, in such places in the village as the temple, the communal well and the village entrance. After the ceremony, a feast is held in the ancestral hall, and a traditional gift of pork is distributed to every male villager."
11 Several immigration sources were examined by the author and archivists at the National Archives in San Bruno including "Return Certificate application case files, 1894-1913," "Wharf Registers of Departures, 1895-1941," partnership files, etc. Other sources, such as "Chinese Passenger Departure Lists, 1882-1914," lack indexes and are on microfilm. I did not conduct an exhaustive search of immigration records.

Figure 48. Joe Pigeon, Bob Lawrence, Jimmie Chow. *Chew Kee Store*

his best friends was a local boy named Bob Lawrence. They remained friends throughout his life.

Like many residents of Fiddletown, he worked with his hands and was able to find jobs in and around Fiddletown. In 1915, he was employed as an assistant in the shop of blacksmith Joseph Pigeon, located just south of the Chew Kee Store. There he learned the skill of a wheelwright, involving heating iron hoops to fit on wagon wheels, and he also learned how to shoe horses, still used for transportation in this rural area. By this time, if not before, he had cut off his queue. After the 1911 Chinese Revolution, it was no longer necessary for males to pay homage to the Qing Dynasty with this hair style. Yet Chow kept his severed braid for the remainder of his life, hidden under his mattress. It is now on exhibit in the Chew Kee Store.

More letters from the family followed. His father at age eighty, wrote that brother Bun Yiu was not doing well and there was no money to send him back home after he had left the village to find work elsewhere. A few years later, a letter came from Bun Yiu informing Chow that their father had died three years before. His brother went on to say that their younger sister had married. All the money was gone and they were living in poverty. At the beginning of the letter, he itemized money that Chow had already sent and then asked for more so that they could survive.

Jimmie Chow had been generous to his family. He had sent more than $100 over time, often in units worth twenty or fifty dollars. The monetary value now of twenty dollars in 1915 is more than $400, and fifty dollars is worth more than $1,000 in 2013—a big sacrifice for Chow who was living on a laborer's wages. Jimmie permanently saved the letters from his family in China, yet he eventually distanced himself from their troubles.

End of a Century

EXODUS OF THE CHINESE FROM AMADOR COUNTY

The years of persecution and discriminatory legislation against the Chinese residents and workers in California had a long-term effect. The population statewide slowly declined from a high of 75,132 in 1880 to 72,472 in 1890, then to 45,753 in 1900. Many returned to China or fled from small towns to cities, especially San Francisco and Sacramento. The Census for Amador County (always an undercount) showed an even more dramatic reduction of Chinese residents: 1,115 in 1880, 324 in 1890, and only 153 in 1900.[1]

As an example, a Chinese funeral in Drytown for Mrs. Foy Sing, who died of consumption in February 1888 was so sparsely attended that "the chief mourner acted as hearse driver, another man sat on the coffin and scattered the funeral papers along the road to the cemetery; two others acted as pall-bearers."[2]

Still, the perception of some whites in Plymouth was that "our Mongolian population is increasing all the time, notwithstanding the statement of Senator Caminetti to the contrary, 'that there was no employment for Chinamen in this county and that they are not employed to any extent.' The Chinamen are getting more numerous and the employment of them by our farmers, in many cases to the exclusion of white men is a fixed fact, much to our disgrace. The hotels are all run by Chinese cooks."[3]

THE GEARY ACT

Another bitter blow was dealt to the Chinese with the passage of the Geary Act in May, 1892. This legislation not only extended the Chinese Exclusion Act for another ten years, but required Chinese residents to obtain a Certificate of Residence from the U.S. government or face deportation. Much like an internal passport, an ID card with two duplicate photographs was required as proof that a Chinese person residing in the U.S. was a legal immigrant. The Chinese were the only ethnicity or race required to carry such papers of identification. It put Chinese in the position of being stopped, searched, jailed and deported. Merchants were

1 Chinn, Thomas, ed. *History of the Chinese in California*, pg. 21. (Chinese Historical Society of America, 1969).
2 *Amador Ledger*, February 22, 1888.
3 *Amador Ledger*, February 2, 1889.

Figure 49. Fanny Mui with children, Ione. *Amador County Archives*

exempted, but still subject to the indignities of being questioned, searched and potentially imprisoned if they could not produce the document.

The Chinese Consolidated Benevolent Association, otherwise known as the Chinese Six Companies, spoke out in protest, calling upon all Chinese in the U.S. to disobey the law and resist registering. Immigrants from China were still citizens of that country which continued to have trade relations with the U.S. The Chinese Six Companies proclaimed that the Geary Act was an unjust and degrading law that violated treaties with China and the rights of Chinese in the U.S. For almost two years, there was wide resistance among the Chinese. The *Amador Ledger* reported on April 7, 1893 regarding the registration deadline of May 5, 1893:

> As the last day approaches in which Chinese can register under the
> Geary Law, they look more glum and sullen. Some of them express
> themselves very bitterly against the law and claim that it will cost

every Chinaman three dollars to register, which is not correct. The rank and file of them, however, seem to plod along as if the 6th of May had no terror for them. It is wonderful how stoically they take this momentous question. The fight is on between the Government and the Six Companies...

The Chinese Six Companies appealed their case to the Supreme Court, but it ruled that the law was constitutional. The newspaper reporter from Ione observed that, "A majority of our citizens are well pleased with the decision of the Court, and the Chinese are correspondingly sad."

It is beyond the scope of this book to write about the broader effects of this law, the reaction of the Chinese government which initiated a trade boycott, and the ensuing violence against Chinese laborers, especially in agricultural communities throughout the state. Suffice it to say, that the government of China capitulated, and consequently, the Chinese Six Companies gave up the fight. The deadline for registration was extended to April 3, 1894.

Notice was given to the Chinese of Amador County that the Deputy Internal Revenue Collector of Chinese registration would visit the towns of Fiddletown (Oleta), Plymouth, Amador City, Jackson, and Ione on successive days in April 1894. Chinese living in other parts of the county were advised to sign up at one of the scheduled places. It is not known how many Chinese people registered. Only two Certificates of Residence from Amador County remain in its archives, and those are from Fiddletown, issued to Chew Kee and Fong Chow Yow.

VISITS TO CHINA

Immigrants from China continued to have many ties to their homeland. They had both personal and business interests back home which prompted occasional visits to China. Because the Scott Act prevented skilled and unskilled laborers from re-entering the U.S., only merchants as a privileged class and U.S. born Chinese had the ability to go and return, although authentication was required.

Merchants and/or those who had a share in their business were required to file "partnership" documents with the immigration service as proof of their exempt status. This document, which required the signatures of at least two white witnesses, allowed them to legally leave and re-enter the U.S under the restrictions of the Chinese Exclusion Act. Some merchants got around the law by having silent partners invest in their business, giving additional people the ability to visit China and return to California.

Figure 50. Wo You partnership application. *National Archives*

In Amador County, members from the businesses of two prominent Ione merchants filed partnership papers. In one example, Wo You, one of the partners of the Hop Wah Chung Company, obtained the testimony of nine white businessmen in Ione for his second trip to China. They swore in a notarized document issued on April 24, 1896 that he had worked for that firm for six years before making a first trip to China in 1894 and that he continued to work there until the present.

The following year Chin Hing Get swore that he and Kai Kee of Ione were the sole partners of Kai Kee and Company. He alone signed the partnership document, which included a paper giving the value of the brick store building as $1,250 and the merchandise in that store as $1,000. This partnership document was submitted so that Kai Kee could make the trip to China.

By the turn of the century, there were a few Chinese families in Amador County with American-born children. If parents could afford it, they traditionally sent the eldest son to China for an education. In 1900, the Mui [Mooey] family of Ione consisted of the father, Ching Ah Mui peddler, age sixty-nine; wife Fanny, thirty-five; two sons, sixteen and eight; and one daughter, four years old. The family decided to send their eldest son Chung to China, most likely to study there. He stayed in China for a few years and in 1913, when he turned twenty years old, Chung applied to re-enter the U.S. By this time, the Angel Island Immigration Station near San Francisco required all Chinese entering the county to be processed and questioned there. Many were detained for months (some for years) until they could either be cleared for entry or deported. Chung Ah Mooey had to produce an Affidavit of Identity to be re-admitted. This document was signed by seven prominent white residents of Ione testifying that they knew him and his mother, Fanny Ah Mooey. Only then could he, an American citizen, return to the U.S.

DECLINE OF CHINATOWNS

By the turn of the century, the communities in Amador County included elderly Chinese people who had lived for decades in California. A few recorded inquests testify to their long presence. You Toy, age sixty-one, worked as a cook in the Olympia Restaurant in Jackson, relocating two years earlier from Fiddletown after her husband returned to China. At the investigation into her death in 1909, a friend from Fiddletown (Oleta) testified that she had known her for about thirty years; another person, Lee Gim, knew her for thirty-four years. Won Tat of Ione, died in January 1911 of consumption and old age. He had lived about forty years in California and died at age seventy-five.

Figure 51. Sixty years in Jackson. *Amador County Archives*

143

It is clear that not all Chinese returned to China. Some chose to remain in the U.S., perhaps because of the availability of work; others stayed because of circumstance, such as not being able to afford the trip back to China. Women, especially, would have had more independence and freedom in the U.S., preferable to their status in China.

Jackson: In Jackson's Chinatown, starting from the late 1880s, there were property sell-offs, many to white Americans. In February of 1888, members of Jackson's Chinese Church were preparing to relocate to Mokelumne Hill in Calaveras County because there were so few Chinese left in Jackson. The next month the lot where the Chinese Church stood was sold to a Caucasian for $600 by the Yan Waah Chinese Company from Mokelumne Hill.

Between 1895 and 1898, the Tung Wa Yee Chow Co. sold two parcels to white Americans where the "old joss house" stood, originally purchased by Chinese twenty years earlier. This Chinese temple in Jackson also must have suffered from lack of membership.

The Jackson Chinatown, described in the press as "the most closely packed and inflammable district of the town," was consumed by fire in July 1901. Apparently caused by the explosion of a kerosene lamp in a Chinese store, the fire destroyed the joss house, a Chinese boarding house, and several other structures, including nearby white businesses. The newspaper reported, "It is impossible to secure a correct estimate of the loss sustained by the Chinese. They lost everything. They had no time to get their money and valuables."[4]

Intentions to rebuild Chinatown were discouraged two weeks later by a bungled attempt to dynamite a structure being built for a Chinese shopkeeper. The person(s) who caused the explosion was not caught, but there were certainly opportunistic interests coveting the properties on north Main Street where Chinatown had been located. More sell-offs continued in the first decade of the twentieth century. Gee Hing bought two lots in 1902 from two long-time Chinese residents, paying $40 for one of the lots. A few months later, for reasons unknown, he turned around and sold the same lot at a loss to for only $10.00 to Domenico Gazarra, who subsequently bought two more lots in Chinatown for the same low price. In another example, Yap Sang purchased half interest in a lot for $200 in 1900 from a Chinese man. Ten years later that same lot was sold by him to a white American for $10.00.

---

4 *Amador Ledger*, July 5, 1901.

The Chinese Masons or the Chi Gung Tong (Zhigongtang) had remained a strong organization in Jackson for many years, but with time it also lost members. The Chinese Masonic Lodge became the last vestige of Jackson's Chinatown. The *Amador Record and Ledger* of March 22, 1927 reported, "From a once flourishing and prosperous section of Celestials it has gradually been reduced until in late years only the old Chinese Masonic Temple and two tumble-down shacks remain. Only a remnant of the former Chinese population is to be found in this city." The property was sold in April 1927 to the Spinetti brothers for $10.00 by remaining members Yip Sing You, Charley Wah Yoo and Ng Fook Yeng. The Chinese Masonic building was slated for demolition, to be replaced by a new store made of brick and reinforced concrete.[5] On Jackson's Main Street all physical traces of its once vibrant Chinatown were gone.

The following year, representatives of the Chi Gung Tong and other Chinese organizations disinterred the bones of the deceased from the Chinese graveyard in Jackson Gate for shipment to China. Only the road name, China Graveyard Road, still denotes the former Chinese cemetery.

The Amador County Museum pays tribute to its former Chinese residents with a large exhibit case containing wide Chinese bamboo hats, brown stoneware jugs, rice wine bottles, a drum and other objects from the Chinese who once lived in Jackson and Amador County.

Ione: In November of 1897, prominent Ione merchants Hop Wah Chung and Kai Kee along with their partners sold the 5.22 acres where Ione's Chinatown was located for $1,000 to other Chinese, Chum Chin and Joe Yow.

Former Ione resident, Joseph Won, born in Ione in 1909, wrote

Figure 52. Joseph Won. *Amador County Archives*

---

5   The new brick building became Spinco's hardware store, currently occupied by Swensen's Footware.

of the last days of its Chinatown. Won lived in Ione until 1926, then left for the city of Stockton, working long hours in a restaurant and studying journalism at night. He noted that there were about thirty-one Chinese left in Chinatown in 1908 and a few dozen others living on ranches. "When I was there, there weren't too many houses. Everybody had a store and lived in it. I lived in a store which had general merchandise, gambling, and whiskey."[6] According to Won, his mother Fannie who was born in Placerville, predicted that Ione's prosperity depended on its pear orchards, which were tended by Chinese workers. Starting in 1911, various owners stopped caring for their orchards. Won related, "The Kai Kees felt the symbolic omen and left in 1912." The following year merchant Hop Wah Chung and his family left Ione.[7] Joseph Won never forgot his roots in Ione and was involved in its homecoming in 1970, "dedicated to the Chinese of our community." In May 1970, the Native Daughters of the Golden West placed a commemorative memorial where Ione's Chinatown once stood at the summit above the town, now overlooking a serene pasture.

Drytown: From its heyday in the 1850s, Drytown slowly contracted in size to 200 people in 1880, of which forty-two were Chinese. By the early twentieth century few Chinese were left. The 1910 Census included two elderly miners and the family of a vegetable peddler Gee (Chin) Ton Louis, consisting of his wife and ten children. His daughters were named Diamond, Ruby and Pearl.[8] Excavations by archeologists conducted in 1986 in a block once occupied by Chinese residents revealed buried pieces of porcelain dinnerware, brown stoneware jars, opium tins and pipe bowls, and other artifacts from daily life. Only these traces remain.

Volcano: Volcano's merchant Sing Kee sold his store property in December 1889, after thirty years in business. One Volcano resident recalled that as children her little brothers would peek into Sing Kee's store. They would find Mr. and Mrs. Sing Kee "in a euphoric state of bliss, smoking opium. They didn't mind the two little boys watching them. They liked children. Sometimes they gave the little fellows a piece of Chinese candy."[9] By 1900 most of the Chinese in Volcano had departed, their "shanties" demolished. The building that housed the Sing Kee Store at Main and Consolation is all that remains of Volcano's Chinatown today.

---

6 *Amador Progress News*, February 1, 1978.
7 *Amador Progress News,* March 31, 1966.
8 Tordoff, *Test Excavations*, pgs. 6-8 and subsequent pages describe the population and excavations in Drytown.
9 Manuscript, Georgia Gillick White, "Walking Tour of Volcano," pg.15-16.

Plymouth never had much of a Chinese population, but in 1882 Ah Ming purchased a building of stone and brick on Old Sacramento Road, where he operated a store. Known to locals as "Old Ming," he apparently kept a vegetable garden behind the store and sold firecrackers as well as general merchandise. He was purportedly killed in an accident around 1920, and his store stands as the only reminder of the Chinese presence in Plymouth. The store was dedicated as a historical monument in August 1970 by Philip Choy, President of the Chinese Historical Society of America in San Francisco.

The Chinese Exclusion Act was made permanent in 1904, severely curtailing immigration of Chinese into the twentieth century and permanently separating husbands in the U.S. from their wives in China. In 1913 California passed the Alien Land Act which prohibited aliens ineligible for citizenship (i.e., the Chinese) from buying or selling land to another ineligible alien. Only Chinese born in the U.S. could obtain citizenship and buy property. In the "land of opportunity," the door was shut. Nonetheless, some enterprising Chinese residents stayed on, found ways to get around the exclusion laws[10] and became successful despite the barriers.

The Chinese Exclusion Act was not repealed until 1943, when the U.S. fought with China against the Japanese in World War II. Much later, the 1965 Immigration Act abolished national quota systems and allowed for the reunification of Chinese families through large-scale immigration.[11]

---

10 The San Francisco earthquake of 1906 destroyed immigration records, allowing some Chinese to claim citizenship. Since children of citizens and merchants were permitted to enter the U.S. from China, the opportunity arose for Chinese Americans to claim unrelated males in China as their progeny, known as "paper sons." Immigration officials at Angel Island conducted intensive interrogations to ferret out those unrelated Chinese, sometimes denying entry to legitimate relatives.

11 Choy, Philip. *The Coming Man*, pg. 172. (Seattle and London, University of Washington Press, 1994).

LAST DAYS OF FIDDLETOWN'S CHINESE COMMUNITY

As the nineteenth century wound down and the new century began, the Chinese community in Fiddletown (Oleta) drew closer together as their numbers declined. The population details for the 1890 U.S. Census are missing due to its destruction by fire. Its absence leaves many questions unanswered about the Chinese population at that time. The 1900 Census itemized only sixteen Chinese out of 450 people residing in Fiddletown. Of the Chinese residents listed, most were in their fifties and sixties, except for Com or Kum Yow, a married woman of forty-six, Fong Chow Yow (Jimmie Chow), age thirteen, and Yee Ayee [Ah Yee], a twenty year old young adult living with her parents.

The remaining Chinese inhabitants obtained whatever day labor they could get. For example, some were employed as woodcutters by Hiram Farnham, long-time resident and owner of a lumber mill that supplied wood to Plymouth. Farnham died in 1896; among the claimants on his estate were Ah Chung, owed $52.65 and Ah Noy, owed $277.30.

The known merchandise stores that remained—Chew Kee, Wo Sing[1], and Lee Kee—continued to sell their wares. The merchant Lee Kee was not listed in any census, but he did appear on extant assessment rolls. The Amador County Assessment Roll for 1892 shows that he owned two properties on both sides of the seasonal creek that delineated Chinatown. One plot included a "garden lot" where vegetables were grown. The following year, in preparation for departure for China, Lee Kee and another partner, Sam Yan filed a partnership document with the immigration service as proof that they were merchants. Three other individuals were listed as partners of Lee Kee & Company, making a total of five. It is unknown whether these were legitimate or silent partners.

Although Chinese laundries were present in most of the towns, including Sutter Creek, in the late nineteenth century, there were none that have been documented in Fiddletown. This may have been because the Chinese in Fiddletown did not offer such services to whites. The village was small and white women were hired for ironing and other tasks.

---

1 Wo Sing is the name of the store, translated by Dr. Ng as "harmony luxuriant." Most early public records refer to the store as Wo Sing & Company. In Chinese, the name appears as Sing Wo, meaning "rising harmony," as listed in the 1896, 1897 and 1903 entries in the *Cemetery Record Book*. These references must be for the same store and proprietor, since there was much stability among Fiddletown Chinese merchants.

Fiddletown's Chinese population was sufficient in the 1890s to hold a grand celebration of the Chinese New Year. Isaac Cooper, a prominent resident of Fiddletown who retired there after a successful real estate career in Iowa, sold eggs and hens to the town's Chinese residents. On February 12, 1892, Cooper wrote in his daily journal:

> Took Fred [grandson] to see the Chinese celebrate the ending of their New Year—firecracker, Rocket, and general tom tom, Cymbals and other performances. Fred fired two bunches of crackers, and was generally pleased, especially, [with] the cooked chickens with their two tail feathers sticking in the birds, and roast and unroasted pigs with oranges in their mouths.

There is some evidence that the Chinese community had a temple. Recalling the main street of town between 1886 through the 1890s, Fiddletown old-timers in the late 1960s mapped a joss house a few doors west of the Chew Kee Store. This location corresponds with *Chung Wah* listed in the 1892 assessment record. Chung Wah means "overseas Chinese" and was the term used by Chinese to refer to the Chinese Consolidated Benevolent Association. The Chong How Association, the Punyu affiliate in Fiddletown since 1871, appeared on state and county tax receipts for 1909 and 1912 in the same location as Chung Wah.

The following year a state and county tax receipt was signed by Chung Wah for China Church, this time two doors east of the Chew Kee Store on property formerly owned by Yee Fung. Unfortunately, no other information has been uncovered that

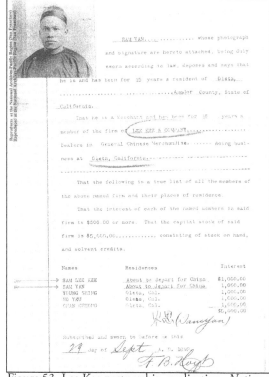

Figure 53. Lee Kee partnership application. *National Archives*

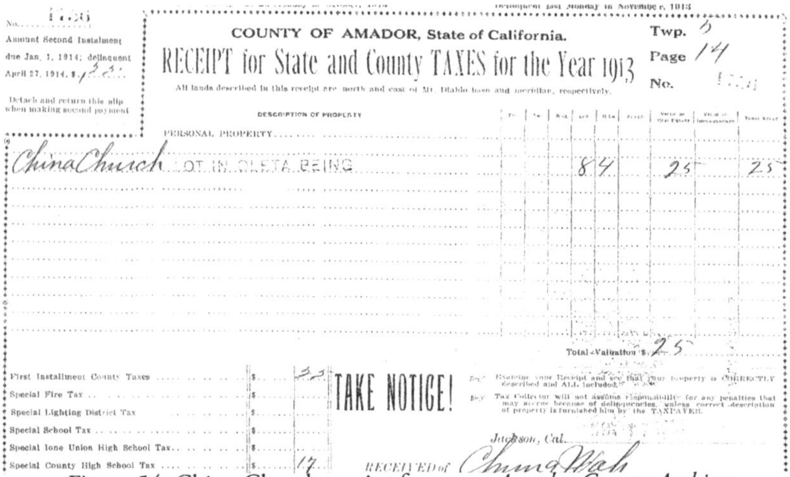
Amount Second Instalment due Jan. 1, 1914; delinquent April 27, 1914. $

Detach and return this slip when making second payment

COUNTY OF AMADOR, State of California.

Twp. 5

RECEIPT for State and County TAXES for the Year 1913

Page 14

No.

All lands described in this receipt are north and east of Mt. Diablo base and meridian, respectively.

DESCRIPTION OF PROPERTY

PERSONAL PROPERTY

China Church LOT IN OLETA, BEING 84 25 25

Total Valuation $ 25

First Installment County Taxes $

Special Fire Tax $

Special Lighting District Tax $

Special School Tax $

Special Ione Union High School Tax $

Special County High School Tax $ 17

TAKE NOTICE!

Examine your Receipt and see that your property is CORRECTLY described and ALL included.

Tax Collector will not assume responsibility for any penalties that may accrue because of delinquencies, unless correct description of property is furnished him by the TAXPAYER.

Jackson, Cal.

RECEIVED of Chung Wah

Figure 54. China Church receipt for taxes. *Amador County Archives*

elaborates on Fiddletown's China Church or connects it with the Chong How Association. Yet the presence of both of these entities in 1912 and 1913 indicates that Fiddletown had a larger Chinese community than recorded in the 1910 Census, in which only four Chinese were listed. A temple in Fiddletown was mentioned in a 1975 book published in Chinese, Liu Bo Chi's *History of Chinese in America*. It is likely that such a close Chinese community would have a place in Fiddletown where its residents could worship deities and revere ancestors.

In the early twentieth century some residents of Fiddletown recalled the few Chinese who remained: Sally" Kum Yow[2], Ah Hawk and mostly, Fong Chow Yow or Jimmie Chow. In 1903 Billie Brown—Fiddletown postmaster, surveyor and blacksmith—purchased the Foo Kee properties, including land west of the seasonal creek. He lived a few lots to the east by his blacksmith shop. Esther Brandt, his granddaughter, later wrote about the Chinese friends of her childhood.[3]

> Just half a block away [from the Brown residence] was Chow Yow, Sally Kum Yow and others of the Chinese family. I was allowed to visit and well remember learning how to roll firecrackers at the hearth of the fireplace inside. I didn't hold the hot Chinese punk away from me and got a burn on my temple leaving a small scar to this day....I remember when Jimmy Chow was going to school and wore a cap and que [sic].

2 In the 1900 Census, Com Yow is listed as a wife, age forty-six living with husband Com Yoke, age sixty-six. In the 1910 Census, Kum Yow is listed as a widow, head of household, and a general laborer, still age forty-six. She may have been living in the store with Chew Kee and a miner, age sixty-eight.

3 Letter from Newport, Oregon addressed to the Fiddletown Preservation Society in the late 1970s.

Then they made him cut off his que or he couldn't go to school. Their grandfather was tall and thin and smoked a tiny white pipe on a long thin curved stem, very delicate, I thought. Then they said he was getting old and wanted to go back to China to die. He wore a long que and a small round cap, the same as Jimmy Chow. He sat most of the day on a chair in the sun in front of the livery stable, so he must have been the caretaker of the stable. Jimmy Chow often helped my grandfather in the blacksmith shop when he was older.

Sally Kum Yow had a pretty sister (I thought they said) who married a man from Stockton....I felt very much in their home even though there were no windows and it took awhile to adjust to the darkness and dimmer glow from fireplace or doorway when inside. They were so nice to me—the beds were like bunk beds and hard wood—no pillows or covers like our beds. Sally was a beautiful gardener and could raise so much better vegetables and berries than my grandfather. He let her raise the garden and shared half with her. Their food always smelled so good when cooking—still my favorite food today, vegetables quick cooked in

Figure 55. Chinese grandfather, possibly Lee Kee. *Amador County Archives*

151

a wok....

I never knew any of them to ever be sick. My grandfather said you could always trust the Chinese—very honest....The family were all well liked and trusted and when it came time for their grandfather to go "home," I felt people in the town helped pay the fare. Sally walked with short steps, both arms up the opposite sleeve of her jacket (like a long jacket) and pants or slacks of a blue-gray color—her hair pulled tight back and in a braid down her back. She helped my grandmother sometimes and came to our house nearly every day.

In the mid-twentieth century, new owners of the property dug up hundreds of shards of Chinese porcelain and pottery in the garden area to the east of the creek. This is the place where Chinese—Sally Kum Yow, Lee Kee and those before them—had raised vegetables. Perhaps as the Chinese departed, it became a disposal site for unwanted dinnerware. On the opposite side of the creek, several large brown earthenware storage jars were discovered in a cellar hole next to stone walls that are carved into the hill on property once owned by Foo Kee. There are two recessed cavities leading to the stone walls, creating areas where Chinese houses may once have stood.

LAST FUNDRAISING FOR THE FIDDLETOWN CEMETERY

Funding and repairing the Chinese cemetery became a major endeavor of the Fiddletown community, even as their numbers dwindled. Fiddletown's Chinese reached out to other Chinese still living in the area for contributions.

In conjunction with the 1903 drive to raise funds for repairing the cemetery, another book, *Donation Records for Restoration of Our Cemetery* was placed in the Chew Kee Store to solicit donations from customers. The text, which has been translated from Chinese reveals a request that is both plaintive and indicative of the community spirit:

> Do good deeds as in sharing food and clothes
> In building bridges and roads
> As time goes by, the fences are going to decay
> Which will affect the tombs of our former friends
> If the fences are not to be repaired soon
> They will be trampled upon by horses and mules
> When thinking of this I cannot help [but be] saddened
> Thus I appeal to my colleagues to get the wooden fences repaired
> While one cannot sustain the adversity himself
> Things can be done with collective effort
> We are now collecting contributions and
> Asking kind-hearted people to help by united efforts to make this a success
> The buried, if having spirit, will surely repay with gratitude

> *Repair project started on the 10th day of the 12th month, in the 29th year of the reign of Emperor Guang Xu (January 16, 1904).*[1]

Contributors in Fiddletown included the associations, Chung Wuo (Zhong He) Association and the Punyu Association, and individual donors Chew Kee, Fong Chow Yow and a few others.

A second copy of the *Donation Records for Restoration of our Cemetery* was placed with the Wui Lei Ho (Hui Li) store in Jackson to encourage donations from its customers. Not only did the store in Jackson

---

1 Translated by Kai Lui, San Francisco, November 2005.

contribute to Fiddletown's cemetery; in addition, many Chinese residents in Jackson donated $1.00 each plus a few who gave smaller amounts. All together, there were twenty-two donors in Jackson, with contributions amounting to $11.60. This copy of the donation book was dated January 31, 1904 (Gui Mao year, fifteenth day of the twelfth month). As an example of how meticulously records were kept, the $11.60 collected from Jackson was correlated and itemized in the *Cemetery Record Book*.

Figure 56. Cover of donation book. *Amador County Archives*

BURIAL IN FIDDLETOWN, RETURN TO CHINA

Yet another book gives important insight into the composition of Fiddletown's Chinese community, the *Record Book of the Deceased* (referred to here as the Fiddletown burial book). This book listed men and women buried in Fiddletown's Chinese cemetery from the 1860s through 1913. It was originally appended to the *Cemetery Record Book* and later copied into a separate volume.

The Fiddletown burial book lists the dead, giving their name, county of origin (men only), date of death according to the Chinese lunar calendar year, Western calendar year of death, and for some entries a puzzling number that may indicate the number of years of residence in California or Fiddletown.[1]

Fifty-one names are recorded in the book, but not in the chronological order of the year of death—a deviation from the way records are kept in the West. The book begins by listing men by county of origin, once more stressing their connection to specific areas of China. Half of them were from the counties of Sze Yup, where so many Chinese originated from. The remaining deceased men were from the county of Heungshan and the three counties of Sam Yup. This is further evidence of the co-existence in Fiddletown of Chinese from different parts of southeastern China.

The first person listed is a Mr. Tse Duk (Xie De) Gong (Gong is a title of respect) from Hoiping County in Sze Yup who died on the twentieth day of the ninth lunar month, eighth year of [Emperor] Guangxu, twenty-three years, Western calendar October 31, 1882. Not only is he the first person in the Fiddletown burial book, but his marble tombstone has been saved and is displayed in the Chew Kee Store. Information from the tombstone is consistent with that in the burial book.

The last person listed was the merchant Ngan Chew Kee. His fate had previously been unknown, but this record confirms that he died in Fiddletown on the eleventh day of the sixth lunar month or July 18, 1913.

Women were listed separately on three pages and their county of origin was not noted. One of the surprises in the list of deceased is the

1 Dr. Sonia Ng translated the *Record Book of the Deceased*, including names of individuals. Based on her conversion of the Chinese lunar calendar, she found discrepancies of a year or more with the Western calendar year listed. For example, with the first person listed, Tse Duk, the Western year of death is 1882, not 1887 as converted in the burial book. David Coates of Oakland translated the tombstone of Tse Duk, also with the 1882 date.

155

number of women who were buried in Fiddletown—twenty-three women, 45 percent of those buried. This number belies the prevailing view that few Chinese women came to California. Of the twenty-three women, over half (fifteen) were single and were probably prostitutes. But their date of death raises many questions because most died in the 1890s and afterwards (the last in 1909). It was very difficult for women to enter the U.S after the Page Act of 1875 and the lives of prostitutes were usually short. Had these women lived in Fiddletown for many years?

Five of the women had the title of "senior madam," an address of respect for elderly ladies. Curiously, three of them died in 1863 and 1864, the earliest death dates recorded in the book. Women brought from China for purposes of prostitution were usually in their teens and early twenties. How and why did these more mature women come to California in the 1850s or 1860s?

Figure 57. Tombstone of Tse Duk. *D. Zorbas*

Three women listed were married. Mrs. Chu or Sigh Choy (Sai Choy) died in 1901, and Mrs. Chiu (Chew) died in 1905. Mrs. Yee died the same year as her husband, Yee Yuke, 1901.[2]

Other men and women with the surname of Yee were listed as deceased, most during the first decade of the twentieth century: Yee Kuan Wo (1896), Miss Yee (1904), Yee Wun (1908), Yee Chow Sung (1908). Yee Sing Wo, who died in 1909, must certainly have been the merchant Sing Wo, also referred to as Wo Sing. All of the Yees were probably from Toishan (Sunning) County in Sze Yup,[3] and may have been in the same clan as the herb doctor, Yee Fung Cheung.

A big puzzle in the Fiddletown burial book is a number that follows the lunar date of death for the entries on the first six pages:

Hoiping County, *Mr. Lau Wai,* 11th day of the 10th month, **22 years**, Western calendar, 1888

Toishan County, *Mr. Wong Yun*, 20th day of the 10th month, **13 years**, Western calendar, 1897

Sunwui County, *Mr. Yeung Chow*, 25th day of the 6th month, **36 years**, Western calendar, 1879

Heungshan County, *Mr. Jeng Ting*, 1st day of the 1st month, **11 years**, Western calendar, 1900

Punyu County, *Mr. Ngan Yun Fook,* 27th day of the 11th month, **14 years**, Western calendar, 1896

Senior Madam Sigh (Sai) Huk, 18th day of the 5th month, **47 years**, Western calendar, 1864

---

2   The Chinese character for the surname of Mrs. Chu differs from the character denoting Ngan Chew's name. Was Sigh Choy married to a different Chu (Chew)? Or was there a second Sigh Choy? The 1900 Census shows Sigh Choy as the wife of (Ngan) Chew Kee. The character for a Mrs Chiu also differs from that of Ngan Chew. Another woman named Yau Choy (older Choy) died in 1909 adding to the confusion of which woman was married to Ngan Chew.
3   In the last three pages of the burial book county of origin is not given for the men. The Yees, men and women, are grouped together on consecutive pages.

Does the number of years refer to the age of the deceased or the number of years spent in the U.S.? If it refers to age, then twelve male children and teens died in the 1890s, an unlikely number of young people given Fiddletown's aging Chinese population. Yet it appears that Senior Madam Sigh Huk could have been forty-seven years old when she died. If the number refers to years of residency, then Mr. Lau Wai came in 1866, a possibility. But there is little likelihood that Mr. Yeung Chow from Sunwui County arrived in 1843.

The burial permit for Mr. Jeng Ting from Heungshan County corresponds with his entry in the Fiddletown burial book.[4] Furthermore, it states his age at the time of death as sixty-four years; therefore, the mysterious number of "11 years" for his entry does not refer to age. It could relate to his time spent in Fiddletown or California. Of course, there is always the possibility of errors in the recording or another interpretation of what the numbers stand for.

The majority of the recorded deaths occurred in the 1890s (twelve men and eleven women) and first decade of the twentieth century (six men, seven women). Were these long time residents of Fiddletown? The few listed in the 1900 Census showed an aging population. The *Record Book of the Deceased* or Fiddletown burial book ends with Chew Kee's death in 1913, and with the death of this important merchant came the final passing of the Chinese community along with its record-keeping.

FINAL RESTING PLACE

Burial in the Fiddletown Chinese Cemetery was temporary. The Chinese have a saying, "Fallen leaves return to their roots." China was the home country of these immigrants and the U.S. did not encourage permanent settlement. The exhumation and shipment of bones was tasked by the district associations or *huiguan* to affiliated county benevolent organizations, known as *sin tong* (*shantang*). The Chong How Benevolent Association, representing the people of Punyu County in southeastern China, was such an organization. Its leaders made arrangements to exhume the bones of the dead, clean, box and label them, and send them from San Francisco to the port of Hong Kong. If the dead were identified, their bones were returned to relatives from their native village where they could be permanently buried and honored. Even the bones of the

4 Dr. Sonia Ng corrected the year of death from Western year 1899 in the burial book to 1900, which also matches the burial permit

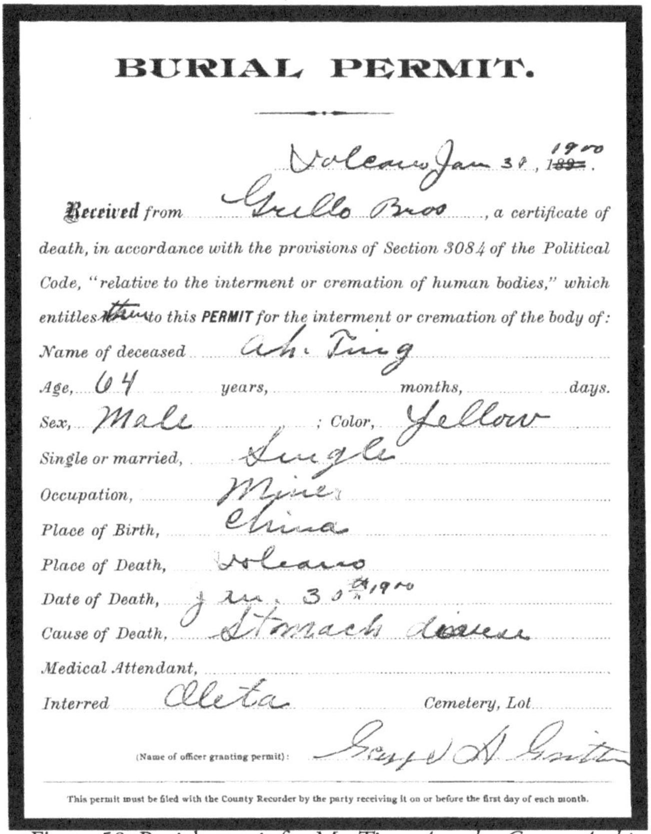

BURIAL PERMIT.

Volcano Jan 31, 1900.

Received from Grillo Bros, a certificate of death, in accordance with the provisions of Section 3084 of the Political Code, "relative to the interment or cremation of human bodies," which entitles them to this **PERMIT** for the interment or cremation of the body of:

Name of deceased Ah. Ting

Age, 64 years, months, days.

Sex, Male ; Color, Yellow

Single or married, Single

Occupation, Miner

Place of Birth, China

Place of Death, Volcano

Date of Death, Jan. 30th, 1900

Cause of Death, Stomach disease

Medical Attendant,

Interred Oleta Cemetery, Lot

(Name of officer granting permit): [illegible]

This permit must be filed with the County Recorder by the party receiving it on or before the first day of each month.

Figure 58. Burial permit for Mr. Ting. *Amador County Archives*

unclaimed and disappeared were accounted for, put in "spirit" boxes, shipped to Hong Kong and placed in charity cemeteries. The district associations collected exit fees from returnees to China and solicited charitable donations to finance the exhumation and shipping of bones.

The Chong How Association completed its first exhumation in 1863 and a second exhumation in 1876. The organization went to great lengths throughout the U.S. and Canadian British Columbia to locate the graves of the deceased.[5] Careful records were kept of those who entered California, those who left for China, and those who died (often reported to the association by fellow countrymen). Each person mattered, and all efforts were made to convey their remains to a final resting place in China.

A very significant discovery from the Chew Kee Store is a combined book which describes the process of shipping the bones to San Francisco

5 "The Second Exhumation and Return of the Remains of Our Departed Friends to the Homeland (1876)" in Judy Yung, ed. *Chinese American Voices: from the Gold Rush to the Present*. (Berkeley, University of California Press, 1999.)

and receiving them in Hong Kong through another organization. Copies of this first edition, *Chong How Tong History of Transporting Bones to San Francisco 1864* and *Hong Kong Gai Sin Tong Account Book for Receiving Bones 1865*, have heretofore not been found. The store contained both the first edition published in 1864 and the third edition from 1893.

A newspaper article, "Wholesale Exhumation," in the April 4, 1863 *Sacramento Daily Union* gives an interesting account of preparation for this first shipment:

> About three hundred Chinese coffins, or boxes, containing the exhumed remains of deceased Chinamen, were yesterday placed on board the schooner *Kate Adams*, for transportation to San Francisco, preparatory to shipment to China. The packages are made of pine lumber, and vary in length from three to seven feet. Some were made of planed lumber, and others of unplaned. Each package was marked with Chinese characters—probably the name, age, etc., of the deceased. A portion of this large shipment was brought to the city by the cars, and the balance were taken from a Chinese house on I street. The remains, it is said, were exhumed in various portions of the State, and have been accumulating for several years past. No shipment of any consequence as to numbers of this character, have taken place from Sacramento during the past three years. The remains of men only are sent back to China, those of women being deemed unworthy of preservation.

As noted before, the Chong How Association was present in Fiddletown and responsible for exhuming the bones of the deceased in its cemetery, usually occurring from two to ten years after a death. The cemetery contained graves of people from different counties who also contributed to the cemetery, but each county *sin tong* was responsible for collecting the bones of their own people.

The *Ledger Dispatch* described an exhumation in Fiddletown in the September 5, 1882 issue: "Last week the Chinese opened twenty-five graves in their cemetery, and sacked the bones and boxed them to send to China. Last Saturday night, on the streets in Chinatown, could be seen the illumination of hundreds of wax candles and the burning of numerous piles of paper [probably for a funeral]." It is perhaps no coincidence that the year of exhumation in Fiddletown was 1882. This is the same year that the Chinese Exclusion Act was passed, signifying growing hostility towards the Chinese.

Fiddletown's last Chinese resident, Fong Chow Yow, better known as Jimmie Chow, talked of a final exhumation in 1917 when the remaining bones in the cemetery were collected.[6] All who were buried in Fiddletown's Chinese cemetery, presumably men and women, were transported and returned to their home country where they could be permanently buried with their ancestors, their spirits finally at rest. Jimmie Chow is the only Chinese buried in Fiddletown's public cemetery.

---

6 Yee, "Anecdotes of Fiddletown."

RENEWAL AND CONTINUITY

JIMMIE CHOW, CHINESE AMERICAN

Jimmie Chow was an American citizen, a voter, a property owner, and a tax payer. In 1908 at age twenty-three he registered to vote as a Republican, and identified himself as a laborer. With the usual confusion over Chinese names, he was listed as Yow, Fong Chow. He registered to vote throughout his life, always as a Republican. For decades, he paid state and local taxes on the adobe Chew Kee Store, and four other parcels, including the gambling house.

WORLD WAR I

Despite the situation that most Chinese were barred from entering the U.S. by the Chinese Exclusion Act, those who were already American citizens were required to register for the draft. In April 1917, the U.S. entered World War I. Chow, now thirty-three years old, was notified by the local draft board in January 1918 that he was classified 1A. The physical examination later that month pronounced him fit and subject to be called into service.

The news of his eligibility to serve in the war was not welcome. Soon after he received the notice, he wrote to his childhood friend Yee, now living in Ripon near the city of Stockton with her husband, Jow Moke. She responded, "Well Chow, I am very sorry that you have been register [sic] if you are over of age." [The age cut-off was initially thirty years.] She advised him to find an attorney or to seek the help of Mr. William "Billie" Brown, a friend of the Chinese in Fiddletown.

Jimmie was able to get the assistance that he needed because the following month, in February, the Adjutant General concluded that "the evidence presented in the case of Fong Chow Yow is sufficient to warrant cancellation of registration." However, in September, 1918, he was again classified 1A. This was the final draft registration and now it encompassed men aged thirty-one to forty-five years old. Chow was never inducted. However, during the war he worked at the U.S. Naval Shipyards at Mare Island near San Francisco where he learned carpentry skills.

One of his schoolmates, Tommy Lott, was drafted and sent abroad to fight. Serving with the American Expeditionary Force, he wrote to "Friend Jimmie" from Kempenich, Germany on February 25, 1919 to let him "know that I haven't forgotten you." He asked how all the boys around town were doing, inquiring about specific people whom they both knew. Wistfully thinking of hunting deer and fishing for trout, he wrote, "I sure can remember some of the good times we had before I left. Guess I will have a few more if nothing happens….Won't be long until the trout season opens so I guess you will be going out after them."

In 1921 "Pal" Grant wrote, inquiring about mutual friends, "I would like to see you Chow and have one or two of those good times that we have had. Hoping this will find you in good health and to hear from you soon." Jimmie had been accepted as one of the guys

CHINESE CONNECTIONS

Jimmie did not abandon his Chinese heritage. He maintained the Chinese diet with purchases of ginger, mushrooms, shrimp and other foodstuff. He ordered Chinese groceries—from Quong Lee & Co. in San Francisco, Hoy Kee & Co. in Sacramento (same store used by Chew Kee) and Fook Chong & Co. in Stockton. His orders were itemized by the stores in Chinese, evidence that Jimmie could read the written Chinese characters. The majority of the documents in the Chew Kee Store are written in Chinese, including letters from his family, invoices sent to him from Chinese groceries and other papers.

Chow was affiliated with the same Chinese organizations that his adopted father, Chew Kee, had also supported. He paid 1932 membership dues to the Chew Yee Association, headquartered in San Francisco, which had reorganized that year to a respectable organization, changing

Figure 59. Letter from Yee to Chow. *Amador County Archives*

its name from the Chew Yee Tong (that had functioned more like a gang) to the Chew Yee Association. The Chong How Benevolent Association, long present in Fiddletown, received donations from Chow, sending him a letter of praise with new year's greetings and wishes that he continue to contribute to the civilization and peace of the home country. He also belonged to the Stockton chapter of the Sam Yup organization in 1932. The receipts for these organizations were written in Chinese, another example of Chow's knowledge of the written language.

Jimmie kept in contact with Yee through letters. His correspondence is lost but several letters from Yee written in English were among the papers found in the store. She addressed him as "dear friend," mentioned the receipt of his "welcome" letters, asking when he planned to come to Stockton to visit. Most of the letters were written between 1917 and 1921 with news about her health, the weather, her husband's employment at Morena Vineyard where he was in charge of over thirty Chinese men, and their older son, Ming.

After 1921, the correspondence appears sporadic, mostly initiated by Yee. In May 1930, she apologetically asked Chow for a loan of fifty dollars. She was looking for a job as cook prior to working in the Manteca Cannery in July. There was desperation in her letter as she wrote, "I need the money by the 25 or 27 of May. Please let me have it. I am shame [sic] to ask you to loan it to me but I got to have it by that time...."[1] Her remaining short letters are from 1944 and 1951. In these last two letters she sent her regards to Elsie Woolfolk, another friend in Fiddletown.

Jimmie had abandoned communicating with his family in China. In 1919 he received a letter in English from a brother named Ah Yin, who wrote, "Chow You, I respectfully to [sic] inform you that I have sent you for [sic] a few letters, but you have no answer for me."[2]

Ten more years passed with no communication from Chow to his brothers. Bun Yiu chided him in 1929 for not writing: "Since you sent the letter with $50 in 1912 which was received, it has been sixteen years that you have not sent a word to us. We don't know how you have been doing and the whole family misses you very much. Please write." He added that he had a fifteen-year-old son in school.[3]

The question remains, "Why did Chow break off communication with his family in China?" According to the only interview with him conducted

---

1 *Chew Kee Store Miscellany* collection. Some letters from Yee are held in this collection; others are at the Amador County Archives.
2 *Chew Kee Store Miscellany, Ethnic Studies Studies Library, UC Berkeley.*
3 Excerpt from letter translated by Dr. Sonia Ng from *Chew Kee Store Miscellany.*

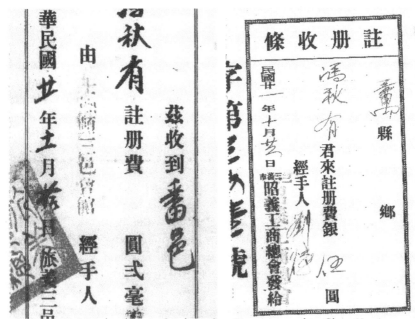

Figure 60. Memberships in Stockton Sam Yup Asso. and in Chew Yee Asso.
Amador County Archives

in 1956 he said, "I have a brother in China. Each Chinese New Year, I send him some money. I haven't heard from him for a while now." This brother must have been Bun Yiu.

Perhaps the ceaseless demands of his family for money were more than he could fulfill, let alone making the long voyage to China. It might have been a question of economics. The pressures for money seemed to be never-ending. He didn't know his natural family except through letters. Were his affections reserved for his adopted father and mother, Chew Kee and Sigh Choy, who raised him? Did his good friends in California mean more to him than his distant family in China? Did he enjoy the freedom and independence of living in rural California, far from traditional family obligations in China? Did he conclude that there was only poverty in China, and he would be better off staying in Fiddletown?

LIFE IN FIDDLETOWN

By 1920 Jimmie was the only Chinese person in town, apart from an elderly 82-year old servant, Ah Hawk, who worked for a local family. Jimmie identified himself in voter registration rolls as a carpenter, and quite a carpenter he was. He built several of the houses in Fiddletown.

Locals referred to him as the "wood butcher." According to one of his friends, he was so good at numbers that "he could figure in his head faster than you could write it out."

Fiddletown was a small rural hamlet, far from population centers, where most people scrambled for a living. It was necessary to be versatile and skilled in a community where survival depended on self-sufficiency. Throughout his life Jimmie worked for just about everybody in town, often working side by side with other Caucasian men in the community—cutting wood, repairing roofs, butchering pigs, hunting—whatever work needed to be done. In the 1940s he worked at the general store as a meat cutter.

Jimmie had moved back into the Chew Kee Store sometime after WWI, sleeping on his hard plank bed, living mostly in the screened

Figure 61. Jimmie Chow's bedroom. *D.Zorbas*

wooden rear part of the building where the two kitchens and his bedroom were. During the winter cold, when Fiddletown had frost and snow, he moved to the storefront, warming himself by the cast-iron wood-burning stove, sitting in a comfortable stuffed chair that he obtained. He brought electricity to the property after it arrived in Fiddletown as late as 1934.[4] In the shed in back of the property, Jimmie raised chickens, as many people in Fiddletown did. He traded eggs for brandy from the merchandise store of Rosenwald & Kahn in nearby Plymouth, six miles west of Fiddletown. Throughout the years, he made only rudimentary changes and minor repairs to the building, which gradually began to deteriorate.

Jimmie did not drive. Several of his friends recalled giving him rides to Sacramento and especially Stockton, where he purchased food and clothing from Chinese stores. One local recalled, "He was a real nice little guy. I gave him rides, many times; other people would give him rides to go to Plymouth, to go to the big city for shopping."

Mary Lawrence, the wife of his close friend Bob, stated in an oral history interview:

> "They wrote up a big thing in the paper about him being lonely.
> Why, he was the most taken care of person you ever met! If some
> person was going to Stockton, say, why they'd stop and pick him
> up and take him along. They probably had lunch together and
> stayed away all day. This was right up to the end. My husband
> [Bob Lawrence] was his very best friend, and he took him to the
> hospital in his last illness."[5]

Still, he must have missed the companionship of a wife and family. Next to his bed, he hung postcards of Western courtship and marriage and several advertisements featuring ladies of fashion adorned the walls of his home in the Chew Kee Store.

Many of the local residents welcomed Jimmie into their homes. Since he was a bachelor, he was often invited for dinner and holidays. One friend remembered, "In fact, he used to eat at our house quite often. My mother would say, 'I'm cooking something that Jimmie likes, go over and tell him to come over for dinner." People from town would bring him their large zucchinis, which he loved to stir-fry on the built-in wok.

In his home Chow was surrounded by objects of the past, left behind by Yee Fung Cheung, Chew Kee, and Sigh Choy: furnishings, utensils,

---

4 Costello, Julia. *Archaeological & Historical Studies at the Chew Kee Store, Fiddletown.* Final Report submitted to the County of Amador. (Foothill Resource Associates, July 1988.)

5 "Mary Lawrence – Postmaster, Fiddletown," interview and transcript by Cedric Clute. Tape #24. (March 1979. Amador County Museum and Amador County Historical Society.)

medical implements, brown stoneware storage jars, bottles, baskets, cigar boxes, cutting blocks, rice bowls, gambling supplies, banners and books in Chinese, newspapers mounted on the walls, and many other traces of work and play from bygone years.

To these, he added his own possessions: carpenter's planes, yearly calendars (some from the Cowan Grocery in Fiddletown, others from banks in San Francisco that catered to Chinese clients), shoe repair tools, crutches, and medicine bottles. Fortunately, he also kept his personal letters, grocery receipts, his draft registration and cancellation, and other papers that help to reconstruct his life and that of the earlier Chinese community. A most frugal man, he mended what he could and hung on to everything else: old newspapers, broken tools, and junk.[6]

As he aged, Jimmie suffered from painful and crippling arthritis. Friends would cut wood for his stove, take him to doctor's appointments and even replaced his leaky roof in the 1950s. Townspeople would

Figure 62. . Jimmie's crutches and pinup calendar. *D. Zorbas*

6 Costello, pg. 42-43.

periodically check up on him. "All the people in Fiddletown were very good to me," he recalled. Several of the locals recalled him with fondness:[7]

> "He seemed to get along with everybody. He'd go up to Randalls' [local hangout] and he'd come in there and he'd mingle with everybody and everything. But he was awful quiet. You'd have to go over there and pinch him to make him talk; otherwise he wouldn't say nothing. He was just taking everything in. He wasn't one of them guys that wanted to be heard all the time. He was a pretty nice guy."

> "He was just like one of us. The guys in those years would go and drink beer and he would drink a soda pop, sitting with all the guys after work. He was a meat cutter and worked in the [general] store for a lot of years. He was a very nice, nice man.

> "He was a shy little gentleman. He led an extremely simple, private life…His home was very austere. No one else could survive in those living conditions. He never complained. He could have moved, but would not."

> "I was privileged to know Jimmie Chow. We met him in his 'twilight of life.' He was a sweet, gentle soul, in spite of the continuous pain he suffered from arthritis. He always greeted us with a broad smile and a welcoming hand! …He never complained, although he had a very difficult life. To this day, his memory makes me smile."

In the 1950s, Jimmie was visited by Dr. Herbert K. Yee, great-grandson of the herb doctor who established the store. From Los Angeles, Johnny Yee of the Chinese Historical Society of Southern California met Chow in 1954 and conducted the only interview with him, describing him as a white-haired man in his 70s, "who graciously invited us into the shop and we had a very interesting and pleasant chat with him."[8] In their conversation, Jimmie mentioned receiving visits from Chinese friends from Stockton and Sacramento, as well as the famous Chinese actress

---

7 Quotations are from correspondence and oral history interviews that I conducted with residents.
8 Yee, "Anecdotes of Fiddletown."

Figure 63. Medicine bottles remain in the store. *D. Zorbas*

Anna May Wong and her sister whom he claimed visited Fiddletown during the summers.[9]

Following a visit to the store from twenty-five teachers from Stockton, Chow related that someone from the California Department of Parks had expressed interest in the Chew Kee Store and that he intended to leave the property to them. However, he sold some artifacts to a collector in the late 1950s and early 1960s which are now in the possession of the Amador County Archives.[10] According to Mary Lawrence, his best friend's wife, "Jimmie Chow sold most of the gambling equipment [from the gambling house across the way]. It was his property....My husband would tell Jimmie that the place could be a museum someday, but Jimmie sold most of the stuff anyway."[11]

---

9 I have not been able to verify Anna May Wong's presence in Fiddletown, although a former resident wrote that as a child she remembered seeing Anna, who would visit occasionally and bring candy for Jimmie to give to the children. According to biographer Graham Russell Hodges, Anna's father, Wo Sing Sam, lived in a "joss (a Chinese medicinal) house in Fiddletown" in his teen years. A postcard from Fiddletown has been found that proclaimed "Anna May Wong's father stayed here." Anna May Wong was born in Los Angeles in 1905. Jimmie Chow was twenty years older than she was.

10 These items were offered on EBay and purchased by Amador County from another party in 2006.

11 Mary Lawrence interview.

Jimmie's arthritis worsened and he was in and out of the hospital. One friend recalled:

> "I visited him in his home. As I said, he had arthritis that would
> really get him in the winter. I'd go in there and pack his wood,
> and build his fires to keep him from freezing to death. He'd get so
> helpless, he could hardly get around."

On April 25, 1965, at age eighty, Jimmie Chow died of leukemia. He left $570, no debts, and no will. Unlike the many Chinese residents who preceded him, he was buried in the Fiddletown public cemetery. His gravestone placed by local residents reads, "Chow Fuong Yow [sic], Native of Fiddletown, Affectionately known as Jimmie Chow."

The legacy of this quiet, frugal, and modest man is in his home, the Chew Kee Store with all its remaining contents—a continuity of more than one hundred years of Chinese living transplanted to this little town, far from the mother country. Just as significant, the life of Jimmie Chow stands as testament of the ability to successfully bestride two very different cultures, working and living as an American while still retaining his Chinese traditions and connections. Fong Chow Yow, or Jimmie Chow, was Chinese American long before the term came into popular use.

THE YEP FAMILY OF JACKSON

Many decades after the demise of Jackson's Chinatown, a sign written in Chinese characters was uncovered during the remodeling of a store the old Chinatown section. The sign was discovered in 1978 by Jackson resident and businessman, Som Yep, who could read Chinese. Nailed to a roof plank, it conveyed the good wishes "prosperity for every family." When the sign was afterwards concealed by a drop ceiling, Yep had it reproduced to perpetuate its good omen.

Som was born in Toishan (Sunning) County, Guangdong in 1915, the eldest son in the family. His father Jimmy had already immigrated to California, working as a potato farmer in the California Delta near Lodi. When he was twelve years old, Som left China to join his father. His mother stayed behind; there were not enough funds to bring her, also, to the U.S. The family situation worsened a few years later when a broken levee flooded the farm and plunged the family into bankruptcy.

Som and his father moved to Jackson in 1932 to operate the kitchen at the historic National Hotel built in 1864. As heirs to one of the world's great cuisines, Chinese immigrants could always survive by cooking and working for restaurants and hotels. Many other avenues of employment were closed because of discrimination. The National Hotel had advertised for three cooks and cook's helpers. By cooking for the hotel, Som's father

Figure 64. May and Som Yep at Sammy's. *Amador County Archives*

ould pay off the debts he had incurred. Father and son did the work of three people and more to keep the hotel kitchen running.

While Som worked in the kitchen, he learned the trade of operating a restaurant. The restaurant business must have been his destiny, because during World War II, Som (known as "Sammy") joined the Army, first serving in the infantry, then designated by a colonel to be a mess sergeant. After all, Som knew how to cook. He became camp cook and trooped all over Italy, using the Italian he had learned in Jackson working with Italian miners and merchants. After the war, he returned to Jackson and continued to work in various restaurants in town. In 1958, Som Yep founded Sammy's Café, which became a local hang-out and institution in Jackson.

Running Sammy's Café was a family affair. Som's wife, May, whom he married in China after the war, became the bookkeeper, girl Friday and occasional waitress. Their children, three sons and one daughter, all worked in the restaurant doing dishes and waiting on tables, sometimes late into the night. Som's family connections in China were not forgotten. As an American citizen, Som, throughout the years, sponsored forty-three relatives to emigrate from China to the U.S. Most of them spoke only Chinese and got their start by working in Sammy's Café. Som's brother-in-law, Art Lee, came to Jackson at age nineteen, became a cook for Sammy's and remained in Jackson for over fifty years.

Sammy's Café was quite the place to be in Jackson. The restaurant served American and Chinese American food, from hamburgers to Chow Mein. It was open for twenty-four hours-a-day, long before that was common practice, meaning hard work and long hours for the staff. All kinds of people patronized Sammy's—farmers, ranchers, local politicians, congressmen, state senators, judges, lawyers, truckers, miners, doctors, travelers and even movie stars. At night, the bar crowd disappeared upstairs to drink and play various card games, such as poker. The actor John Wayne and director John Ford joined in the card games when filming in the area. Although gambling was illegal then, it continued to be tolerated in Jackson.

Som became a prominent businessman in Jackson and a friend of many people. In 1972, at age fifty-seven, he was elected to the Jackson City Council, getting more votes than any other candidate.[1] He served two years on the council, resigning because of business pressures.[2] He

---

1 *Amador Dispatch*, April 5, 1972 and *Amador Ledger*, April 13, 1972
2 *Amador Dispatch*, August 21, 1974

was most proud of helping to build the Jackson Civic Center.

In 1985, Som retired and relocated to Sacramento. His wife's brother and sister-in law, who came from Toishan in 1979, purchased and operated the restaurant for about seven years, their three children also working in the restaurant. For many years a group of local businessmen and politicians would meet for coffee every weekday just before 10:00 a.m. and again at 3:00 p.m., flipping quarters to see who would buy coffee for all. In 1985, the 10-to-10 Coffee Club, as they were known, celebrated the anniversary of meeting at Sammy's for almost thirty years.

Sammy's Café is no longer a feature of Jackson life. Som Yep died in 2009.[3] However, his children, grandchildren and all the people he and May helped come to the U.S. have made a life in this country. The racial barriers to immigration, employment, marriage, and housing have been removed. Som and May's son, niece, and their children continue to live in Jackson.

---

3 *Amador Ledger Dispatch*, "Obituaries: Som Yep" February 17, 2009.

THE YEE FAMILY LEGACY

Yee Fung Cheung's eldest son (Yee Lun Wo) never left China since he had the primary responsibility of caring for elderly parents. Instead, he sent his nine year old son, Yee Way Duk, to Sacramento in 1906 to live with his uncle, Yee Lok Sam, also known as T. Wah Hing. The boy, who adopted the Western name Henry Yee, was tutored by his uncle in the practice of herbal medicine and went to school in Sacramento. At a time when few Chinese people could enter the U.S., Chinese students were allowed to immigrate and avail themselves of American educational opportunities. Henry attended university at Stanford, U.C. Berkeley, and received an M.S. in civil engineering from the University of Michigan.

Henry Yee returned to China for a number of years, where he served as Director of Public Works in Guangdong Province, eventually becoming Chief Engineer for the Canton-Swatow Railroad. A Chinese person could not possibly have achieved the same thing in the U.S. during that time. Political turmoil in China brought him back to Sacramento in 1929, along with his wife and five children. Unable to find work as an engineer because of discrimination against the Chinese, he applied the skills in herbal medicine learnt as a young man, setting up his business at 707 J Street in the same Sacramento building where his uncle and grandfather, Yee Fung Cheung had practiced. Henry Yee became a leader in Chinese American associations and involved in several Sacramento community organizations.

From there, the Yee success story continues. Yee Fung Cheung's descendants—those of his son, Yee Lok Sam, and grandson, Dr. Henry Yee—became prominent herbalists, doctors, and dentists in Sacramento and Stockton. The family of Yee Fung Cheung is now in its seventh generation in California. The dentistry office at 707 J. Street in Sacramento is still used by Dr. Wesley Yee, great-great-grandson of Yee Fung Cheung.

Dr. Herbert K. Yee followed in his father Henry's footsteps, excelling in his profession (dentistry) and as a leader in community service.[1] The recipient of many awards and honors, he also created a scholarship fund for deserving dental students at his alma mater, the University of the Pacific in Stockton. He has never forgotten his heritage, both in Fiddletown and in China.[2] Like other Cantonese who prospered in the U.S., he became a

1 "Herbert K Yee Rises to 1996 International College of Dentists Presidency, *ICD Key*, 1996; "Herbert K. Yee: a Man for All Seasons," *Land Park News*, February 26, 1998.
2 Thompson, Willard and Ruth, "Roots—The Saga of a Chinese-American Family Here," *Sacramento Bee*, September 18, 1988.

Figure 65. Herbert K. Yee in front of dedication plaques at Chew Kee Store.

benefactor to his village of origin in China, Sing Tong Village in Toishan County, where in 1981 he sponsored the building of a new elementary school that serves 400 students from six adjoining villages. He also became the first Asian member of the Sacramento Pioneer Association.

Dr. Herbert K. Yee related the following in an interview:[3]

> We revered our ancestors, my parents, etc, and as such our reverence extended to the original Yee that came from China over a hundred years ago, who walked, slept, worked, and played in that little building in Fiddletown. One just can't help but feel that, if that was torn down or destroyed….that part of me will be destroyed also. For we have considered that building [to be] a symbol of our roots.

Dr. Yee and his wife Inez have become benefactors to Fiddletown in many ways, actively preserving its Chinatown and generously contributing funds for restoring the Chew Kee Store and the Chinese

3 Wey, "Oral HistoryInterview," 1978.

Gambling House. His sons and their families continue to be involved with Fiddletown.

PRESERVING THE CHINESE HERITAGE IN FIDDLETOWN

Ownership of the Chew Kee Store and Chinese Gambling House

After Jimmie Chow died in 1965, the Chew Kee property was appraised at $1,400. Because Chow had no written will or known heirs, his estate was distributed by law to the State of California. The Fiddletown Preservation Society, which was formed in 1964 to save the town's one-room schoolhouse, urged Amador County to purchase both the Chew Kee Store and the Chinese Gambling House, about to be sold at public auction by the state. There was even danger that the store would be demolished. Albert Schoonover, spokesman for the Preservation Society and aware of the rarity of the rammed earth store and its contents, proposed that the county accept the buildings as historic sites; the group would operate the Chew Kee Store as a museum. Consequently, in the process of obtaining the buildings, the County of Amador signed an agreement in June 1967 with the Fiddletown Preservation Society in which the organization would operate and open the two "Jimmie Chow Buildings" on a limited basis.

Figure 66. Chew Kee Store before restoration. *Amador County Archives*

179

The Chew Kee Store was dedicated as a historic site on February 24, 1968, with sponsorship from the Fiddletown Preservation Society and Amador County's History and Landmarks Committee. The historian Philip Choy, of the Chinese Historical Society of America in San Francisco, participated in a ceremony that was attended by two hundred people, many of Chinese ancestry. Among other things, the Chew Kee Store was singled out as a rammed earth adobe, a building technique common in China but unique in California. It was at this time that the press perpetuated the story that Fiddletown's Chinatown was once second in size to that of San Francisco.

Meanwhile, members of the Fiddletown Preservation Society had begun to sort through the piles of paper (including newspapers amassed by Chow) and thousands of objects, cleaning and organizing artifacts for display. Chinese historians, including Philip Choy and members of the Chinese Historical Society of America, identified some of the valuable and unique books written in Chinese. A few dedicated volunteers intermittently opened the store as a museum on weekends and for group visits.

Ownership and survival of the Chew Kee Store became precarious on two fronts. In 1975, the Amador County Treasurer-Tax Collector conveyed the property to the State of California for non-payment of 1966 property taxes, amounting to $14.54. Before the store could be sold at public auction, the county would have the option to again acquire it. In addition, because the Chew Kee Store was part of a larger parcel never separately deeded, its title was unclear. It took many years in court for the complexity of ownership to be sorted out and resolved. The Fiddletown Preservation Society continued to assume responsibility for the store and its precious contents while these matters were worked out.

LIMESTONE QUARRY CONTROVERSY

The other threat to the store was even more serious. Fiddletown's historic structures were potentially imperiled by a limestone quarry proposed in 1974 by a Colorado company, Ideal Basic Industries (also known as Ideal Cement Company), on land three miles southeast of Fiddletown. Plans were to extract 150,000 tons of limestone per year, transported in 36-ton trucks through Fiddletown's narrow Main Street. At peak activity, these trucks would rumble through town every six to ten minutes, their vibrations endangering historic structures, especially

Fiddletown's Chinese buildings. The quarry was to be strip-mined over a period of forty-five years.

The Fiddletown Preservation Society, consisting of concerned members (none of whom were Chinese), embarked on a campaign to oppose the quarry, citing additional concerns of noise, dust, air pollution, and safety on Main Street. The organization filed a lawsuit to halt county approval of the quarry, joined by the Amador County Historical Society.[1] For over four years, the Fiddletown Preservation Society fought the project. The community of Fiddletown was divided between those who supported the quarry and those who opposed it. The controversy was covered by newspapers in Sacramento, San Francisco and even Los Angeles. Finally at the end of May 1978, the Amador County Planning Commission turned down the project permit at a meeting attended by three hundred people, featuring an impassioned plea by Dr. Herbert K. Yee, a letter of opposition by California Secretary of State March Fong Eu, and a rousing speech from a representative from the Conference of Historical Societies.[2]

A proposal a few months later from Ideal Basic Industries to build a bypass haul road through the middle of Fiddletown's historic Chinese cemetery drew more opposition, this time from Chinese organizations.[3] Faced with more controversy and more expense, Ideal abandoned the project. The preservationists of Fiddletown, a small community of about 112 people, had won the battle.

HISTORIC DISTRICT OF FIDDLETOWN: NATIONAL REGISTER STATUS

At the same time that they were contesting the quarry, members of the Fiddletown Preservation Society, led by president Marie Scofield, nominated the town for the National Register of Historic Places. Hopes were that this would pave the way for grant monies to preserve and renovate the town's historic buildings, as well as prohibit the use of federal funds for widening the road. On June 7, 1978, Fiddletown was formally acknowledged by the National Park Service as a historic district with eighteen historically significant sites. Several buildings constructed

1 "Court Suit Filed in Move to Halt Fiddletown Quarry," *Amador Dispatch*, October 9, 1974.

2 "It's all Over for the Quarry," May 31, 1978, *Amador Progress-News*, pg. A-3.

3 "Old Cemeteries Fall Prey to Time, Vandals," *Los Angeles Times*, July 16, 1978, part 1.

in the 1850s and 1860s were included, among them the Chew Kee Store, the Chinese Gambling House, the privately owned Chinese adobe and the Chinese General Store (the Foo Kee General Store).

While the limestone controversy was going on, an initial inventory of the contents of the Chew Kee Store had begun under a grant awarded in December 1977 by the Chinese Historical Society of Southern California to Nancy Wey, who held a Ph.D. in Oriental Art and was fascinated by the store.[4] Wey did not meet the terms of the contract, but she was successful in publicizing both the priceless contents of Chew Kee Store and the life of Jimmie Chow in several newspapers, including the *San Francisco Examiner and Chronicle*, which published her article, "Fiddletown's Chinese Past," on July 29, 1979. In this and earlier articles for the *Amador Dispatch*, Wey postulated that Jimmie never left Fiddletown for better opportunity because he considered himself the caretaker, not the owner of the store, aiming to preserve it for future generations.[5] She described Jimmie as a solitary and lonely person who "didn't alter the interior to make the store more comfortable for himself; the only modern convenience is electricity." Indeed, Jimmie was a packrat, but he lived in the store, made a few alterations, added items of his own, and even sold some of the artifacts. Furthermore, he had many good friends.

The store was cleaned, remaining objects arranged, and in 1980 was opened on weekends as a museum under the auspices of the Fiddletown Preservation Society. However, the condition of the building was of serious concern, and the back wooden rooms added to the store by Chew Kee and Sigh Choy were not included in tours.

RESTORATION OF THE CHEW KEE STORE

Restoration of the Chew Kee Store did not begin until 1987, more than twenty years after Jimmie Chow died. As early as fall 1984, Dr. Herbert K. Yee alerted the Amador County Board of Supervisors and Fiddletown Preservation Society that grant funds were available through California's Proposition 18 (California Park and Recreational Facilities Act) to arrest the deterioration of the Chew Kee Store. "I hope that we can all join together in preserving this landmark of great significance

---

4 *Nancy Wey Papers*, including research project materials concerning Fiddletown, are held by the Ethnic Studies Library, University of California, Berkeley.
5 Dunne, Mike, "Why Did Jimmy Chow Stay Behind?," *Amador Dispatch*, June 7, 1978.; Dunne, Mike, "Jimmy Chow Had a Dream—And It Might Come True," *Sacramento Bee*, June ? 1978.

Figure 67. Chew Kee Store in 2008. *D. Zorbas*

from disintegrating and thus preserve a rich Chinese cultural heritage for succeeding generations to enjoy and to find a sense of pride in."[6]

Under the auspices of Amador County, the Fiddletown Preservation Society was awarded a grant which brought in $88,000 from the California Department of Parks and Recreation Department's Office of Historic Preservation, matched by $10,000 from Dr. Herbert K. Yee. The Fiddletown Preservation Society and Chinese organizations contributed an additional $2,000. The partners of the cultural resource management firm of Foothill Resources, Ltd, archeologist Dr. Julia Costello and architectural historian Judith Marvin, were instrumental in writing the grant and directing all aspects of the restoration project.

Prior to reconstruction of the rear wooden portion of the building—the two kitchens and Jimmie Chow's bedroom and living area—were emptied of their many contents, which were inventoried, cataloged, and individually photographed. Archeological excavations were conducted around the building's perimeter to construct a French drain that would carry destructive groundwater away from the adobe walls. Artifacts retrieved from this process included fragments or sherds of Chinese porcelain and stoneware, opium tins, and bottle glass.

6 Correspondence, Herbert K. Yee to Amador County Board of Supervisors and Fiddletown Preservation Society, October 18, 1984 and November 16, 1984.

The entire project included building a new shake roof, stabilizing and repairing rammed earth walls, restoring and reattaching the wooden additions, repairing sheds and other work that was carried out by David Easton of Rammed Earth Works.[7] The change in roofline to its historic steep-pitch provoked criticism from some locals who were used to its appearance in the 1950s, when the roof was first repaired. However, both the roof and building restoration revealed much about the original rammed earth construction.

More grant money to conserve collections at the Chew Kee Store and the Amador County Museum was obtained from the federal government's Institute of Museum and Library Services that same year. The grant application, written by historian Judith Marvin, stated that "the Chew Kee Store is not only the single most important holding of the Amador County Museum, but it is an acknowledged treasure of California and the West." A description of conservation needs was conducted by experts from the Oakland Museum and as a result, archeologist Jane Russell along with volunteers accomplished an inventory of the objects inside the store, a daunting task considering the thousands of artifacts accumulated over more than a century. However, the dire need to protect and conserve these objects and the interior of the store—the topic of another grant—has yet to be funded.

Restoration work on the Chew Kee Store structure was finished in 1987 thanks to the efforts of engineers, archeologists, members of the Fiddletown Preservation Society, Marvin's and Costello's students from San Joaquin Delta College in Stockton[8] and many volunteers. In addition, herbs and medicinal contents assembled in drawers by Dr. Yee Fung Cheung were identified by students from the University of the Pacific, School of Pharmacy, with help from Chinese pharmacist relatives living in China.

During the project, the restoration of the Chew Kee Store received wide publicity. The story of its occupants—the herb doctor Yee Fung Cheung, the merchant Chew Kee, Sigh Choy and especially Jimmie Chow—along with recognition of its historic importance were expressed

7 For more details on the project, see Costello, Julia G. *Archaeological & Historical Studies at the Chew Kee Store, Fiddletown.* (Final Report Submitted to the County of Amador, Foothill Resource Associates, July 1988.)
8 Students were involved in cataloging and photographing artifacts though a Museum Studies class conducted by Judith Marvin at San Joaquin Delta College and involved in archeological excavations through an Archeological Studies class taught by Julia Costello at the same college.

in many newspaper articles. In May 1989 the Fiddletown Preservation Society and the Yee Family Association received a special commendation from Governor of California George Deukmejian for the preservation of the Chew Kee Store. The Governor wrote, "The Fiddletown Preservation Society is further commended for its steadfast stewardship and dedication in the preservation of an uniquely significant resource with its rammed earth adobe construction technique housing an irreplaceable 19th century Chinese herbal medicine collection."

THE ROCS PROJECT: RESTORATION OF GAMBLING HOUSE AND CHINESE GENERAL STORE

Two other historic buildings remaining from Fiddletown's Chinatown were critically endangered, deteriorating to the point of collapse. These buildings, once an integral part of Chinatown, complemented the Chew Kee Store. The Chinese Gambling House had been called "hazardous and dangerous" by the Amador County Building Director in 1975. Although members of the Fiddletown Preservation Society replaced the roof with tin and repaired the floors that year, no preservation work had followed. Both buildings were constructed in the late 1850s or early 1860s. Chinese laborers built the gambling house, its rear wall consisting of the

Figure 68. Herbert and Inez Yee presenting ROCS check to author with grandson Darren, daughter-in-law Karun, and son Doug on right.

185

Figure 69. Mason Leland Peterson restoring Gambling House. *E. Zorbas*

sloping hillside. Each building had a loft—used by the Foo Kee store for merchandise storage, and possibly used by the gambling house for entertainment by sing-song girls.

By the new millennium, the front brick facing of the Chinese Gambling House was pulling away from its stone walls. The Chinese General Store had huge fissures in the brick beneath its front windows, and the entire structure was unstable. Although the latter building was in private hands, its owners—Dick Stanley and Anne Hellman—were convinced that such a resource should be under public ownership. The building was donated by them to Amador County, which accepted the two-story Chinese General Store in year 2000 with the assurance that the Fiddletown Preservation Society would apply on the county's behalf for grants to preserve the building.

The Fiddletown Preservation Society named their project to preserve the two Chinese buildings ROCS (*Restoration of Chinese Buildings*). With Amador County's participation and grant writing by Judith Marvin, an allowance of $203,200 from the California Heritage Fund Grant Program (Proposition 12), under the California Office of Historic Preservation, was awarded in November 2002. Since this was a matching grant, the next few years were spent on an intensive campaign to create awareness and raise money for the project. An annual Chinese Heritage Day organized first in 2005 by members of the Fiddletown Preservation Society, featured presentations, book-signing, music, and demonstrations of Chinese culture that attracted Chinese and other people from Sacramento, the San Francisco Bay Area and nearby counties.

Smaller grants were received from local and Chinese organizations, as well as donations from generous individuals, including Dr. Herbert K. Yee. In a competitive bidding process, Garavalia Architecture, Inc. of San Francisco was the recipient in 2006 of the contract to preserve the two imperiled structures. Unlike the Chew Kee Store, the Chinese store and gambling house were empty inside, except for gambling house walls covered with newspaper insulation, removed during the project. These rare buildings presented challenges that required knowledge of building techniques from the mid-19th century.

It was only after a state grant of $208,000 was received in 2008 from a highly competitive program, CCHE or the California Cultural & Historical Endowment (Proposition 40), that the match was made and construction could go forward. Project Managers Carl McDanel and Jack Feichtner from the Fiddletown Preservation Society oversaw the project budget and development, guided by plans prepared by Garavaglia Architecture, Inc. The two fragile buildings had suffered major damage from water and time and, like the Chew Kee Store, required special drains. Expert masons replaced missing and eroding bricks— handmade in a different era—with old bricks and mortar compatible with the original materials. Some walls were completely rebuilt and both roofs were replaced. To raise additional funds toward the end of the project, the Fiddletown Preservation Society's Brick-by-Brick campaign encouraged individuals and Chinese organizations to purchase memorial bricks, now displayed in a monument adjacent to the Gambling House. At the conclusion of the ROCS project, the Amador County Board of Supervisors advanced funds, later reimbursed with grant money, which covered final expenses.

The first phase of the ROCS project, entailing stabilizing and weatherproofing the buildings was completed by the end of 2008. Once again, the Fiddletown Preservation Society received the Governor's Historic Preservation Award (2010) as well as the California Preservation Foundation's 2009 Preservation Design Award, along with commendations for architect Michael Garavaglia, principal of the firm.

The California Cultural & Historical Endowment recognized the significance of Fiddletown's Chinese buildings as a rare example of a Gold Rush-era Chinatown that demonstrates the contribution of Chinese immigrants to California history and culture. Although work on the exterior of the Chinese Gambling House and Chinese General Store is completed, the next phase of the Fiddletown ROCS project aims at making them into interpretive museums that will continue to tell the story of Chinese presence during and after the Gold Rush.

LEGACY OF FIDDLETOWN CHINATOWN

Fiddletown's Chew Kee Store is a time capsule that reflects over one hundred years of Chinese life as experienced by its occupants: Dr. Yee Fung Cheung, Chew Kee, Sigh Choy, and Jimmie Chow. Everything in the store was constructed, imported, used by the people who lived there; nothing new has been added. The store now operates as a museum, open Saturday afternoons from April through October. Visitors are amazed and enthralled with the ambiance and array of objects and furnishings—from elaborately decorated tea boxes to Jimmie Chow's queue. Everything in the various rooms of the store is on display, evoking a home as well as a former Chinese commercial enterprise.

The Chinese Gambling House and the Chinese General Store are open only for special events in Fiddletown. Their interiors still require structural upgrading in order to be safe for public use. The interiors also need to be upgraded for modern display of artifacts, including objects excavated by archeologists from around the buildings.

As of the writing of this book, it has been twenty-six years since preservation work was undertaken for the Chew Kee Store. The building is showing large cracks on interior walls and the roof is in need of replacement. Major conservation work by experts is required to clean and preserve deteriorating paper, textiles and other artifacts, and to protect the

Figure 70. Chinese Gambling Hall and General Store after restoration. *E. Zorbas*

entire store interior from decay. The structure and the objects within are in jeopardy.

Fiddletown is the only community in California where a cluster of Gold Rush buildings connected with Chinese immigrants is still standing. The Chew Kee Store is an authentic record of Chinese life, a legacy from the California Gold Rush that resonates with all who visit. It is unique, a historical treasure that cannot be lost.

Since the financial crisis of 2008, government grant money for preservation, especially from California bonds, is scarce. The Fiddletown Preservation Society is a small dedicated group that in the past has managed to save the structures in its imperiled Chinatown. Now it needs help if the legacy is to survive.

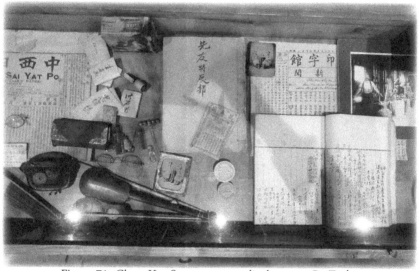

Figure 71. Chew Kee Store museum display case. *D. Zorbas*

POSTSCRIPT

BEGINNINGS: My Path to Fiddletown
Chinatown

I have been asked by Chinese Americans why I am so interested in the Chinese and their history in the U.S. This personal essay attempts to explain my interest and fascination.

This book begins with dreams and obsession. I never thought that my path would bring my husband and me from the Los Angeles area to the little village of Fiddletown where we purchased a long-abandoned orchard and vineyard in 1987, the realization of a dream of owning land in a rural area. Our discovery of the former gold rush town of Fiddletown in the Sierra Nevada foothills presented the opportunity to meld interests and skills that had been dormant, waiting for synthesis.

My love of history began in university, where I specialized in European history, it continued with Civil War studies in graduate school, and was honed at the Pasadena Public Library. There along with other research librarians, I discovered the joys of delving into local history. The desire to write was awaiting a subject.

When I first visited Fiddletown's Chew Kee Store, I entered another world, a world unknown to me. I was captivated by baskets hanging from the ceiling, the large brown stoneware jars, the rows of herb drawers labeled with Chinese characters, the altar with incense and strange gods, the inscrutable red banners written in black Chinese characters, the many medicine bottles, the back rooms with beds made of wooden planks, the office with an abacus and Chinese carved wooden stamps, the kitchens with dishware and utensils from China. There were so many objects, mostly unfamiliar, that spoke of the lives of the Chinese people who had lived in the store. I learned about the herb doctor, the first resident, and Jimmie Chow, the last Chinese in Fiddletown and the store's last occupant. But there was so much that I didn't know—who were these Chinese immigrants, why were they here in the first place, why did they settle in Fiddletown, and how come none are left? Where did they go and why?

I wanted to know more about the Chinese, but realized that before I could embark on that quest, I needed to know about Fiddletown's history. After all, this was a town created by the Gold Rush, a town that had once been full of activity and people but was now a quiet unpopulated village in the hills, off the beaten track. So my first step was learning about Fiddletown as well as California history. I began by interviewing several elders in Fiddletown, a process that gave me deep respect for rural people who learned to be self-sufficient, enjoying the comfort of a close community while lacking many modern amenities. For my book *Fiddletown: From Gold Rush to Rediscovery*, I included two chapters about the Chinese who lived in Fiddletown. I knew that there was more to learn.

I started by reading published histories about the Chinese experience in California, moved by the perseverance of Chinese immigrants and appalled by the discrimination against them, something that touched me deeply. Why do people who are perceived as different become the objects of racial, religious or ethnic hatred? How did this dark side of human nature play out locally in Fiddletown and Amador County?

Once we relocated to Fiddletown in 2001, I had the opportunity to become involved with the Fiddletown Preservation Society, which provides docents to staff the Chew Kee Store museum. I also began volunteering at the Amador County Archives, containing a wealth of documents from the county's past. As a docent, volunteer and later a board member of the Fiddletown Preservation Society, I was able to spend time in the herb store, scrutinizing its many artifacts and absorbing its ambience. Chinese culture was a mystery to me, something needing exploration.

When I was shown a trunk in the Chew Kee Store filled with receipts, envelopes, letters, slips of paper and many books, most written in Chinese, I knew there was more to the Chew Kee story. Whereas the store's artifacts had been documented by archeologists, most of the manuscripts written in Chinese had not been translated or closely examined. With the consent of the Fiddletown Preservation Society, in 2003 I transferred the majority of the paper items from the store to the county archives for cataloging and long-term preservation. The items also included personal and official documents, photographs, and memorabilia that belonged to Jimmie Chow.

Thereafter, I became obsessed about finding out all I could about the Chinese people who had lived in Fiddletown and Amador County. At the County Recorder's office, I searched for every deed issued between the 1850s and 1920s to any person with a Chinese name. At the Amador County Archives, I looked up every document dealing with the Chinese, from bills issued by court translators to inquests. I used the handwritten index of the *Amador Ledger* newspaper compiled by County Archivist

Larry Cenotto to read relevant news articles and editorials written about the county's Chinese population.

Meanwhile, I became involved with the Fiddletown Preservation Society's efforts to preserve the two of the town's structures on the verge of collapse, Chinese Gambling House and Chinese General Store. I joined Chinese American organizations in Sacramento to learn more about the culture and to create awareness of the condition of Fiddletown's Chinese buildings. I also participated in fundraising, writing grants and organizing special events honoring Fiddletown's Chinese heritage.

From 2003 to 2006, I searched for people who could translate the written material in Chinese. Some assistance came from members in the Sacramento Chinese Culture Foundation, who helped with translations of a few items, including an important letter. I was also referred to a professional translator, who decoded copies of other items, including excerpts from books found in the store. All of the translators thus far had been speakers of Mandarin, very different from the Cantonese spoken by Chinese immigrants. The written characters are the same in both languages, but the nuances and interpretations are different. I nabbed a young teacher visiting from Guangdong Province who was fascinated with the Chew Kee Store. She agreed to translate some unidentified papers, which turned out to be mostly business transactions. So much still remained to be translated, and I could not find anybody who would come and join me at the Amador County Archives to examine the entire collection of the Chinese books and documents there.

I also started writing about the Chinese in Fiddletown and Amador County. The thought of writing another book seemed daunting, and after writing an article and a few chapters, I became discouraged, lacking self-confidence to continue. I felt that I really hadn't achieved an insight into Chinese culture.

In 2008, I made the exciting discovery that the University of California at Berkeley had acquired and cataloged Chinese items from Fiddletown, identified as *Chew Kee Store Miscellany: Fiddletown, Amador County, Calif., 1882-1928*. The collection consisted of correspondence and documents, including letters to Fong Chow Yow (Jimmie Chow) from his father and brother. At my first opportunity, I visited the Ethnic Studies Library on the Berkeley campus. There I was allowed to examine two archival boxes containing originals of the letters to Chow. My excitement could hardly be contained as I handled the manuscripts, even though I was unable to read Chinese. Some letters had been translated anonymously, many more were unidentified. Here was a trove of personal letters from China! I had to know what was written and by whom.

I enlisted the help of the eminent Chinese American historian, Philip Choy in San Francisco. He was then working with a woman from Guangdong who was assisting him with translations of other materials. But how could I to get the letters to him? I found out that the Ethnic Studies Library had microfilm copies of the Chew Kee Store material. A neighbor in Fiddletown worked in an office next to the library and kindly offered to look at the microfilm and make printed copies. Since the contents of the reel were in Chinese, he numbered the first thirty pages for identification. I later purchased the two reels of microfilm so I could make prints locally of the remaining letters.

In 2008 and 2009 Philip Choy and Yuet Ho Tsui examined the Chow letters, providing me with translations of the most important ones. Furthermore, Philip provided insight to the Chinese in nineteenth century California, observing that only a person familiar with Chinese American history and the Cantonese language could give the proper interpretation of the written materials. He explained the complicated trajectory of letters sent from villages in Guangdong to their final destination, travelling from Hong Kong to San Francisco to one or more Chinese stores until they reached recipients working in the mining regions. Phil accompanied me to the National Archives in San Bruno where we searched records to determine if Chow went to China, as his family implored him to do in their letters from "home." We found no conclusive evidence, but I was obsessed and continued to search.

Based on new information revealed in the letters, I shared the story of Jimmie Chow with the docents at the Chew Kee Store, wrote an article for historical journals (never published), and gave presentations for Fiddletown's Heritage Day event. For the next two years I was stalled by health and personal issues from continuing to write about Fiddletown's Chinese community.

My breakthrough arrived in 2013 and it was worth the long journey. I was introduced by Fiddletown's archeologist, Jane Russell, to Sonia Ng, professional translator and historian of Chinese in the U.S. Sonia had visited the Chew Kee Store and was very impressed by its contents. Upon hearing that I was researching and writing about Fiddletown's Chinese, Sonia was eager to meet me. Subsequently she has come several times from the Bay Area to Fiddletown, usually bearing homemade noodles. Finally, I had found someone proficient in Cantonese to accompany me to the archives, to examine the materials I had photocopied, to review translations, to translate books that had lain unopened for decades. Many of the books are unique, giving a rare glimpse into the activities of the Chinese immigrants who ventured far from their homeland. More than providing translations, Sonia explained many facets of Chinese culture and customs that gave a context for all the written materials. In Sonia I found a person both curious and knowledgeable. We share enthusiasm for the Chinese experience in the U.S., a love of history, preservation and food. This book is written because of her guidance and encouragement. It has been a wonderful collaboration.

ACKNOWLEDGEMENTS

The Amador County Archives was my home base for research, offering a rich array of documents, maps and photographs that contain the history of the county and its residents. As a longtime volunteer there, I had access to its wonderful collection. I am grateful to the late Archivist, Larry Cenotto who created the county archives, former Archivist Deborah Cook, former Records Manager Lisa Hopkins who improved the organization of the archives, and Teresa Guidi, current Records Manager and caring custodian of this great resource. After the Chew Kee collection was transferred from the store to the county archives, Larry Cenotto accessioned the individual papers and photos, giving public access through the archives' online catalog. His loan to me of his hand-written index to the *Amador Ledger* was invaluable.

I spent many an hour searching deeds at the Amador County Recorder's Office, where I was greatly assisted by Tico Arnese, Elaine Lackey, and Debbie Ryan. The Amador County Library in Jackson is also an important resource, both for its newspaper collection on microfilm, access online to Ancestry.com, and its efficient interlibrary loan service, thanks to Linda Laolagi.

Several people were most generous in sharing resources they gathered about the Chinese. They include archeologist Jane Russell, historian and writer JoAnn Levy, archeologist Kimberly Wooten and historians and writers, Carolyn Fregulia and Eric Costa. Mathematician Dick Stanley was generous with his time by sharing with me his Fiddletown maps and kindly printing out Chinese language documents on microfilm from the Ethnic Studies Library at UC Berkeley, a tedious task that is much appreciated.

I thank the Bancroft Library and particularly the Ethnic Studies Library at the University of California, Berkeley for permission to reproduce material from their collections. Asian American Studies librarians Wei Chi Poon (retired) and currently, Sine Hwang Jensen, have been most cooperative. Archivists Bill Greene and Marisa Louie at the National Archives in San Bruno were informative and helpful.

Artist Ron Scofield, photographers Daniel D'Agostini, and Laura Faye Mah kindly gave me permission to reproduce their artwork. The majority of the photographs in the book came from the Amador County Archives, largely from the Chew Kee Store collection, and from photos taken my husband, Dimitri. In addition, graphic material is reproduced courtesy of the Huntington Library, the Book Club of California (from their reprint of the *Miner's Own Book*), and the Ethnic Studies Library at UC Berkeley.

My appreciation goes to many people, whom I interviewed about Jimmie Chow: the Yee family, especially Dr. Herbert K. Yee; the Yep family, especially James Yep; Fiddletown residents Nancy Germolis, George and Esther Woolfolk, Coleen Fine Randolph, Mitch Lubenko, as well as Delbert Glavich, Julius Albiani, Bryan Lynch, Mary Lawrence, Clarence Randall and Charlie Tyler—all departed. In written notes, Audrey Shelander and Dianne Deaver Frutos provided additional insights.

The translations of the letters from Jimmie Chow's family in the *Chew Kee Store Miscellany* collection were vital and for that effort, I thank Vicki Beaton and Chung Kong; Selia Tan when visiting from Gwangdong; and Kai Lui, paid with funds from the Fiddletown Preservation Society. As noted in the previous chapter, historian Philip Choy (aided by Yuet Ho Tsui) went beyond translation by answering my many questions, explaining the cultural context, and accompanying me to the National Archives in San Bruno. I am very grateful for his interest in Fiddletown's Chew Kee Store and his patience with me.

My highest accolades go to Dr. Sonia Ng, professional translator and historian, fellow enthusiast of Chinese America, collaborator and friend. Sonia opened the door to decoding the many publications in Chinese from the Chew Kee Store, including the books found there. Her translations of the very important *Cemetery Record Book* and the *Record Book of the Deceased* from Fiddletown are critical to an understanding of its Chinese community. In addition to translating, Sonia reviewed many of the chapters that I wrote, acting as editor and cheerleader while enlightening me about Cantonese culture transposed in California. Her support was absolutely essential to the writing of this book.

I am also very fortunate to have had a professional editor, Marj Stuart, work with me. Marj carefully scrutinized the entire book, refining sentences, correcting punctuation, and always striving to improve clarity of expression. Also a friend with a great sense of humor, Marj was wonderful to collaborate with.

My husband Dimitri—a man of many talents and abilities: writer, photographer, farmer, superb cook, magician with everything technical— was steadfast and encouraging during this long process. To him, I owe the transformation of the manuscript into book form, the design of the book and many of the photographs within. He was most cooperative in accommodating all the illustrative material as well as my many requests for revisions. I am grateful to him for his skill in all aspects of computer software, his enduring love and willingness to be my publisher.

Finally, I must thank all those involved in the preservation of Fiddletown's Chinatown, including the support of Amador County with grant requests and the acquisition of the Chinese General Store. Julia Costello and Judith Marvin of Foothill Resources, Ltd. have continued their interest in Fiddletown, lending their professional expertise, including writing grants, and volunteering many hours for both the Chew Kee Store restoration and the ROCS project. We in Fiddletown are fortunate to have their participation. Members of the Fiddletown Preservation Society who were involved in the Fiddletown ROCS project included Jack and Sheila Feichtner, Carl and Marilyn McDanel, Larry Oliphant, Roger Nunn, Beth Squire, Marie Scofield, Lynda Phillips, Mary Kwoka, and Scott Baxter. Commendations to all of them as well as to Renee Chapman for writing the CCHE grant and to Gwen Bohdan for coordinating the Chinese Heritage events. The dedicated docents, led by Judi Kinser, who staff the Chew Kee Store museum, also deserve my heartfelt thanks.

Elaine Zorbas

RESOURCES

MAPS

Map 1.   California counties

202

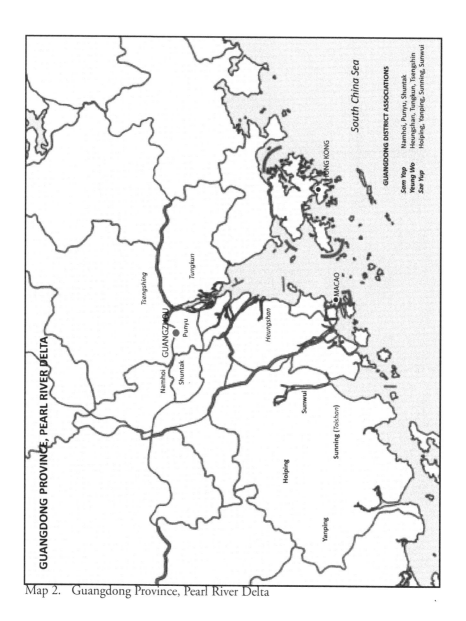

Map 2.   Guangdong Province, Pearl River Delta

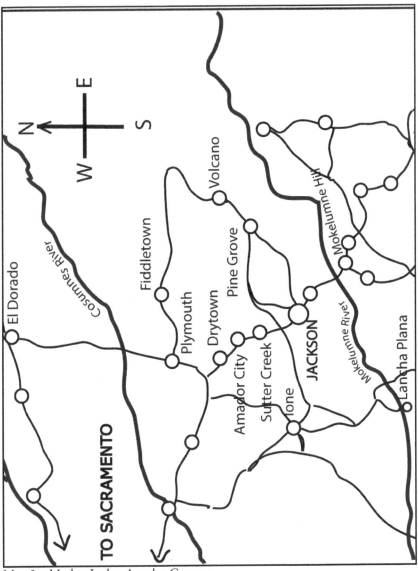

Map 3.   Mother Lode - Amador County

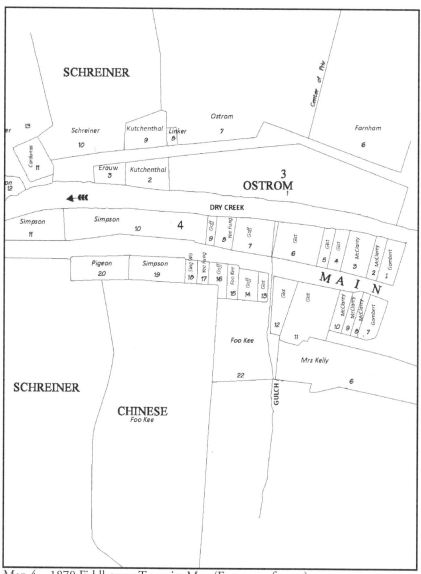

Map 4.   1870 Fiddletown Townsite Map (East part of town)

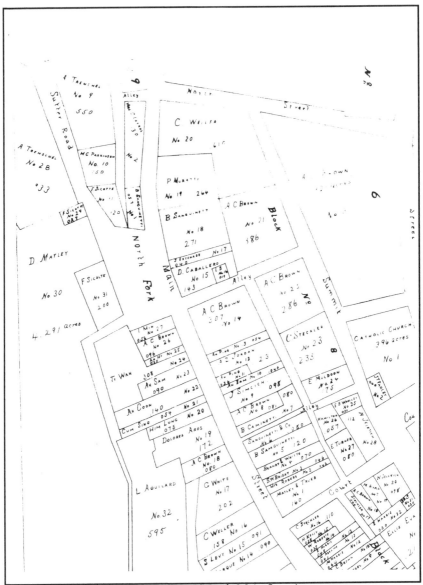

Map 5.   1870 Jackson Townsite Map (North Main Street)

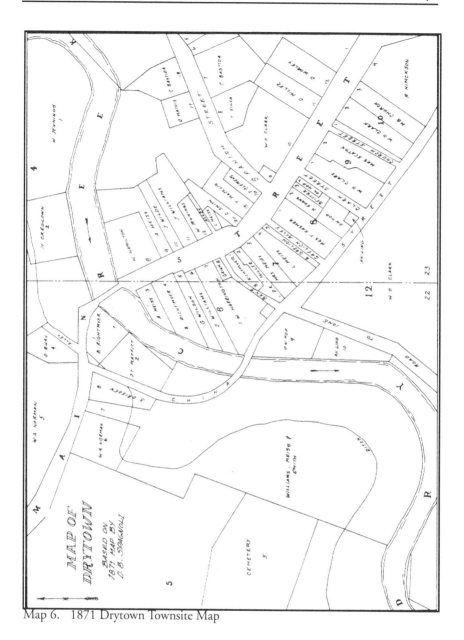

Map 6.   1871 Drytown Townsite Map

BIBLIOGRAPHY

Ball, J. Dyer. *Things Chinese, or Notes Connected with China.* London, John Murray, 1926.

Barlow, Jeffrey and Christine Richardson. *China Doctor of John Day.* Portland, Binford & Mort, 1979.

Bloomfield, Frena. *The Book of Chinese Beliefs.* N.Y. Ballantine Books, 1983.

Cenotto, Larry. *Logan's Alley: Amador County Yesterdays in Picture and Prose.* 5 vols. Jackson, Cenotto Publications, 1988-2006.

Chan, Sucheng. *This Bitter-Sweet Soil: The Chinese in California Agriculture, 1860-1910.* Berkeley, University of California Press, 1986.

Chan, Sucheung, ed. *Chinese American Transnationalism: The Flow of People, Resources, and Ideas between China and America during the Exclusion Era.* Philadelphia, Temple University Press, 2006.

Chan, Sucheng, ed. *Entry Denied: Exclusion and the Chinese Community in America, 1882-1943.* Philadelphia, Temple University Press, 1991.

Chinn, Thomas, ed. *History of the Chinese in California.* San Francisco, Chinese Historical Society of America, 1969.

Choy, Philip P. *Canton Footprints: Sacramento's Chinese Legacy.* Sacramento, Chinese American Council of Sacramento, 2007.

Choy, Philip, Lorraine Dong, and Marlon K. Hom, ed. *The Coming Man: 19th Century American Perceptions of the Chinese.* Seattle and London, University of Washington Press, 1994.

Chang, Jung. *Empress Dowager Cixi.* New York, Alfred A. Knopf, 2013.

Chung, Sue Fawn and Priscilla Wegars, ed. *Chinese American Death Rituals: Respecting the Ancestors.* Lanham, MD, Altamira Press, 2005.

Chung, Sue Fawn. *In Pursuit of Gold: Chinese American Miners and Merchants in the American West.* Urbana, University of Illinois Press, 2011.

Cook, Deborah Coleen. *Ione and the Jackson Valley.* Arcadia Publishing, Charleston, SC, 2008.

Cook, Deborah Coleen. *Jackson.* Arcadia Publishing, Charleston, SC, 2007.

Dillon, Michael. *China: A Modern History.* London, B. Tauris, 2010.

Doble, John. *John Doble's Journal and Letters from the Mines: Mokelumne Hill, Jackson, Volcano, and San Francisco, 1851-1865.*

Denver, Old West Publishing Co., 1962.

Doré, Henry. *Chinese Customs*. Singapore, Graham Brash Publishers, 1987. First published in French in 1911.

Doten, Alfred. *The Journals of Alfred Doten, 1849-1903*. edited by Walter Van Tilberg Clark. Reno, Nevada, University of Nevada Press, 1973.

Farkas, Lani Ah Tye. *Bury my Bones in America*. Nevada City, Carl Mautz Publishing, 1998.

Fregulia, Carolyn. *Italians of the Gold Country*. Charleston, SC, Arcadia Publishing, 2007.

Gong, Rosemary. *Good Luck Life: The Essential Guide to Chinese American Celebrations and Culture*. New York, HarperCollins, 2005.

A History of the Sam Yup Benevolent Association in the United States. San Francisco, Sum Yup Benevolent Association History Editorial Committee, 2000.

Hittell, John S. and James W. Marshall, Edwin G. Waite. *The Discovery of Gold in California*. Palo Alto, Lewis Osborne, 1968.

Hoexter, Corinne K. *From Canton to California*. NewYork, Four Winds Press, 1976.

Hodges, Graham Russell Gao. *Anna May Wong: From Laundryman's Daughter to Hollywood Legend*. Palgrave, 2004.

Hom, Marlon K. *Songs of Gold Mountain: Cantonese Rhymes from San Francisco Chinatown*. Berkeley, University of California Press, 1987.

Hsu, Madeline. *Dreaming of Gold, Dreaming of Home: Transnationalism and Migration Between the United States and South China, 1882-1943*. Stanford, Ca, Stanford University Press, 2000.

Lai, Him Mark, "Historical Development of the Chinese Consolidated Benevolent Association/Huiguan System. In *Chinese America: History and Perspectives, Chinese Historical Society of America*, 1987.

Lai, Him Mark, Genny Lim, and Judy Yung. *Island: Poetry and History of Chinese Immigrants on Angel Island, 1910-1940*. Seattle and London, University of Washington Press, 1991.

Lee, Rose Hum. *The Chinese in the United States of America*. Hong Kong University Press (Oxford University Press), 1960.

[Mason], Jesse D. *History of Amador County, California*. Oakland, Thompson & West, 1881.

The Miner's Own Book, Containing Correct Illustrations and Descriptions of the Various Modes of California Mining. 1858. Reprint with an Introduction by Rodman W. Paul. San Francisco, The Book Club of California, 1949.

Minnick, Sylvia Sun. *Samfow: the San Joaquin Chinese Legacy.* Fresno, Panorma West Publishing, 1988.

Reid, Daniel P. *Chinese Herbal Medicine.* Boston, Shambala Publications, 1987.

Roberts, John A.G. *A History of China.* 2d. ed. Palgrave, 2006.

Sandmeyer, Elmer Clarence. *The Anti-Chinese Movement in California.* Urbana, University of Illinois, 1939,1973.

Schwarz, Henry G., ed. *Chinese Medicine on the Golden Mountain: an Interpretive Guide.* Seattle, Wing Luke Memorial Museum, 1984.

Sinn, Elizabeth. *Pacific Crossing: California Gold, Chinese Migration, and the Making of Hong Kong.* Hong Kong, Hong Kong University Press, 2013.

Spence, Jonathan D. *The Search for Modern China.* 2d ed. New York, W.W. Norton, 1999.

Stepanchuk, Carol and Charles Wong. *Mooncakes and Hungry Ghosts.* San Francisco, China Books & Periodicals, 1991.

Sung, Betty Lee. *Mountain of Gold: the Story of the Chinese in America.* New York, Macmillan, 1967.

Sung, Vivien. *Five-Fold Happiness: Chinese Concepts of Luck, Prosperity, Longevity, Happiness and Wealth.* San Francisco, Chronicle Books, 2002.

Taylor, Bayard. *El Dorado or Adventures in the Path of Empire.* New York, Alfred A. Knopf, 1949.

Tong, Benson. *Unsubmissive Women: Chinese Prostitutes in Nineteenth Century San Francisco.* Norman, University of Oklahoma Press, 1994.

Yee, Johnny. "Anecdotes of Fiddletown." In *1978 Souvenir Book. Los Angeles Chinatown.* Los Angeles, Chinese Chamber of Commerce.

Yung, Judy, Gordon H. Chang, Him Mark Lai, ed. *Chinese American Voices: From the Gold Rush to the Present.* Berkeley, University of California, 2006.

Yung, Judy. *Unbound Feet: A Social History of Chinese Women in San Francisco.* Berkeley, University of California Press, 1995.

Yung, Judy. *Unbound Voices: A Documentary History of Chinese Women in San Francisco.* Berkeley, University of California Press, 1999.

Wegars, Priscilla, ed. *Hidden Heritage: Historical Archaeology of the Overseas Chinese.* Amityville, New York, Baywood Publishing

Company, Inc., 1993.

Williams, Stephen. *The Chinese in the California Mines, 1848-1860.* San Francisco, R and E Research Associations, 1971.

DIGITAL SOURCES

http://cdnc.ucr.edu/cgi-bin/cdnc (newspapers on California Digital Archive)

http://www.cinarc.org/Freemasons.html#anchor_219: *Chinese Secret Societies/"Freemasons"*

http:/ faculty.lls.edu/manheim/cl1/Chinese (California Constitution, Article XIX 1879)

http://freemasonry.bcy.ca/history/chinese_freemasons/index.html

http://www.imdb.com/name/nm0938923/bio (Anna May Wong)

http://immigrationinamerica.org/395-burlingame-treaty-of-1868.html

http:// oregonstate.edu/cla/polisci/sahr/sahr

http://en.wikipedia.org/wiki/Opium

http://en.wikipedia.org/wiki/Anna May Wong

PERIODICAL ARTICLES, THESES, REPORTS

"An Analysis of the Chinese Question consisting of a Special Message of the Governor, and, in Reply Thereto, Two Letters of the Chinamen, and a Memorial of the Citizens of San Francisco." San Francisco, *San Francisco Herald*, 1852.

Clebsch, William A. "Goodness Gold, and God: The California Mining Career of Peter Y. Cool, 1851-2." In *Pacific Historian*, 1966 Summer Issue, pg. 19-42. Includes transcription of Peter Cool's pocket day book from the collection of the Henry E. Huntington Library, San Marino, California.

Costello, Julia G. "An Archive of Artifacts: The Chew Kee Store." *Pacific Discovery*, Spring 1989.

Costello, Julia G. "Archaeological & Historical Studies at the Chew Kee Store, Fiddletown." Final Report Submitted to the County of Amador, Foothill Resource Associates, July 1988.

Cullin, Stewart. "The Gambling Games of the Chinese in America," *Philology Literature and Archaeology*, Vol. 1, no. 4, 1891 reprinted www. gamesmuseum.uwaterloo.ca/Archives/Culin/Gambling1891/index.html

Dunstan, Roger. "Gambling in California," Chapter 1.Sacramento,

California State Library, California Research Bureau, 2007

Heaney, Thomas, "By the Sword Still Sheathed: The Miners, the Militia, and the Amador War of 1871." Paper for History 191, Sacramento State, fall 1989.

Heaney, Thomas, "From Frontier to Company Mill Town: Sutter Creek, 1851-1881." Thesis, California State University, Sacramento, 1993.

"Herbert K. Yee: A man for all seasons." *Land Park News*, February 26, 1998, pg. 1

"Herbert J. Yee Rises to 1996 International College of Dentists Presidency." *ICD Key*, 1996

Lane, Stuart C. "A History of Volcano, Amador County from the Gold Rush to the Seventies" Master's thesis, California State University, Sacramento, 1959.

Murder of M.V.B. Griswold by Five Chinese Assassins. Jackson, T.A. Springer & Company, 1858. A copy is held at the Amador County Archives.

Russell, Jane. "An Ethnohistorical and Archaeological Examination of the Chew Kee (Store), Fiddletown, California." Master's thesis, California State University, Sacramento, 1991.

Thompson, Willard and Ruth. "Roots— the Saga of a Chinese-American Family Here." *Sacramento Bee*, September 18, 1988.

Tordoff, Judith D., "Test Excavations at the Block 8 Site, Ca-Ama-305/H Locus A, Drytown, Amador County, California," Sacramento, The Hornet Foundation of California State University, Sacramento, California for the California Department of Transportation, February, 1987.

Yee, Franklin, "The Contribution of the Yee Family to Chinese Medicine in Fiddletown and Sacramento: Yin, Yang, and the Yees." Unpublished paper for Fiddletown's second Annual Chinese Heritage Celebration, April 1, 2006.

Yee, Franklin, "The Chinese Doctor's Role." *Sierra Sacramento Valley Medicine*, March/April, 2004.

INTERVIEWS

"James Yep, telephone interviews, September 5, 2006 and March 5, 2014

Munden Michel, telephone interview, March 4, 2014

Daniel and Art Lee, telephone conversation, April 5, 2013 and July

21, 2013.

Mary Lawrence – Postmaster, Fiddletown," interview and transcript by Cedric Clute. Tape #24, March 1979. Amador County Museum and Amador County Historical Society.

Wey, Nancy. "Oral History Interview with Dr. Herbert Yee, Great-Grandson of Dr. Fan-Chung Yee." June 4, 1978. Transcript of tape recording. *Nancy Wey Papers*, Ethnic Studies Library, University of California, Berkeley.

Yee, Herbert K. "Speech to Sacramento Historical Society." January 16, 1988. Sacramento, Sun Yat Sen Memorial Hall. Transcription of tape recording.

ARCHIVAL SOURCES

Amador County.
  Assessment Records, 1855, 1856, 1878, 1892
  Indexes to Assessment Rolls, 1881-1889
  Board of Supervisors Minutes, October 1854-May 1855
  Business licenses, 1863-1870
  Deeds and Grantee-Grantor Index, 1854-1920
  Inquests
  Judges Certificates, 1870, 1871
  Justice Returns in Criminal Cases, 1864-1865
  Probate Records (selected)
  Road Overseer's Reports, 1860s
  Township Maps, 1870-1871
Amador County District Court, 11th Judicial District, Yee Lung, vs. Sutter Canal & Mining Company, E. Ginocchio, etc., "Deposition for Proof of Debt No. 1, Claim of Ye Lung,"
Chew Kee Store Miscellany collection, Ethnic Studies Library, University of California, Berkeley
Chinese language books and documents from the Chew Kee Store and Amador County Archives
Isaac Cooper Journal, 1891-1892. [unpublished]
Payroll of Men Employed by the Oneida Mining Co., September, 1871- February 1878
Spencer Richard's Letter to his friend Warren, Fiddletown, June 26, 1855(?), Bancroft Library, University of California, Berkeley, BANC MSS C-B 547:26

U.S. Census of Population, Amador County, 1860-1930

INDEX

A

Ah Choy 91
Ah Gin 122
Ah Hawk 150, 166
Ah Ming 56
Ah Moke 38, 39
Ah Poon 39
Alien Land Act 147
Altars 47, 106, 113
Amador City 9, 32, 68
Amador County 15, 20, 29, 32, 56, 68, 71, 75, 179, 186
  Board of Supervisors 182, 187
  Chinese population 37, 63, 92, 139
  History and Landmarks Committee 180
Amador County Historical Society 181
Amador County Laborer's Association. See Miners' League
Amador County Museum 34, 145, 184
Amador War 65
American Flat Gravel Company 77
Angel Island Immigration Station 143
Angel's Camp 19
Anti-Chinese associations 74
Anti-Chinese Convention 74
Anti-Chinese movement 67, 71
Archeology
  Excavations 55, 97, 146, 183, 188
Arson
  Drytown 33
  Fiddletown 73, 81
  Jackson 70, 73, 144
Arthur, Chester A. (President) 72
Atkinson, Charles 81

B

Bak Gup Pil 99, 118
Barge, George 122
Big Bar 16, 18
Bigler, John 18
Bing Su Yut Ming 133

Boxer Rebellion 120
Boycotts 68, 74, 82
Brandt, Esther 150
Briggs, R.M. 24
Brown, Billie 124, 150, 163
Bun Yiu 131, 133, 136, 165
Burial 27, 86, 109, 145, 155
Burlingame Treaty 63

C

Calaveras County 8, 19
California
  Chinese population 139
California constitution 70
California Cultural & Historical Endowment 187
California Department of Parks and Recreation
  Grants 183
California Heritage Fund Grant Program 186
California Office of Historic Preservation 183, 186
Caminetti, Anthony 74, 139
Canton City. See Guangzhou
Cantonese language 4, 105, 128
Canton Province. See Guangdong Province
Canton-Swatow Railroad 176
Carbondale Coal Mine 66
Carvalho, Charles T. 24
Cemeteries
  Amador County 110
  Fiddletown 112, 153, 155, 181
  Jackson 106, 111
Central Pacific Railroad 49, 63
Certificates of Residence 128, 139
Charitable donations 88, 113, 153
Cheung How Cheung 118
Chew Kee 62, 79, 89, 96, 114, 117, 126, 141, 148, 155, 164, 166, 184
  Debts 121
Chew Kee Store 34, 40, 41, 46, 52, 82, 106, 122, 128, 167, 168, 172, 177, 180, 182, 188
  Awards 185
  Books 88, 112, 118, 120, 153, 155
  Grants 182
  Museum 34, 188
  Preservation 184

Chew Yee Association 164
Chew Yee Tong 86
Chichizola, Augustine 32
Chico 68
Chi Gong Tong 87
Chi Gung Tong 106, 145
China 11, 71, 84, 103, 120, 127, 131, 135, 155, 158, 166
  Religion 105
  Revolution 124, 133, 136
  Secret societies 87
  Treaties 63, 72, 140
China Church
  Fiddletown 149
China Graveyard Road 34, 145
Chinese adobe
  Fiddletown 59
Chinese Camp 24, 26, 54
Chinese Church
  Jackson 107, 144
Chinese Consolidated Benevolent Association 140, 149. See also Chinese Six
      Companies
Chinese credit union 114
Chinese diet 43, 55, 59, 164
Chinese Exclusion Act 71, 80, 91, 128, 139, 147, 160
Chinese Gambling House 34, 179, 182, 188
  Restoration 186
Chinese gardens 32, 51, 53, 60
Chinese General Store 34, 182, 188
  Fiddletown 58
  Restoration 186
Chinese grocery stores 164
Chinese Historical Society of America 147, 180
Chinese Historical Society of Southern California 170, 182
Chinese households 94, 95, 142
Chinese immigrants 12, 77, 106, 114
Chinese immigration 18, 70, 71, 74, 139, 147
Chinese laborers 20, 63, 66, 93, 141
Chinese language 4
  Newspapers 120, 125
Chinese Masonic Lodge, Jackson 86
Chinese Masons. See Chi Gung Tong
Chinese medicine 43
Chinese New Year 47, 61, 102, 128, 149, 166
Chinese organizations. See District associations

Chinese Six Companies 13, 24, 140
Chinese society 13
Chong How Benevolent Association 85, 149, 158, 165
Chou Yee 23, 24, 26, 28
Chow, Jimmie 150, 160, 163, 179, 182, 184. See also Fong Chow Yow
  Family correspondence 165
  Occupation 136, 166
Chow Yow. See Fong Chow Yow
Choy, Philip 50, 147, 180, 195
Chung Wuo Association 153
Clear Brightness Festival 109
Clinton 68
Columbia 19
Conference of Historical Societies 181
Confucian values 13, 27
Coon See 24
Coon You 24, 28
Cooper, Isaac 149
Costello, Julia 183
Cosumnes Mining and Ditching Company 17
Cosumnes River 8, 16, 17, 20
Cowan Grocery, Fiddletown 169
Crime 29, 30

D

Davis, Mary Kane 38
Davis, Stephen 38
Deukmejian, George (Governor) 185
District associations 12, 30, 84, 102, 158
District feuds 85
Doss, John 39
Doten, Alfred 18
Dragon Boat Festival 103
Dry Creek 35
Drytown 9, 15, 19, 29, 30, 32, 33, 91, 139, 146
  Chinese population 33, 52, 63
  Property ownership 52

E

Easton, David 184
El Dorado County 8
Eu, March Fong 181
Exclusion. See Chinese Exclusion Act

Exhumation. See Burial
Exports. See Trade
Expulsion of Chinese 19, 70, 73

F

Families 95
Fan Tan 100
Farnham, Hiram 148
Feichtner, Jack 187
Feng shui 41, 112
Fiddletown 10, 17, 32, 34, 35, 89, 102, 128, 167, 177
  Chinese population 37, 63, 71, 77, 79, 93, 98, 148
  National Register of Historic Places 181
  Property ownership 39, 51, 59
Fiddletown Preservation Society 179, 181, 183
  Awards 185, 187
Fiddletown ROCS project 186, 188
Fong Chow Yow 120, 125, 141, 148. See also Chow, Jimmie
  Adoption 130
  Family letters 131, 136
Foo Kee 51, 57, 58, 77, 89, 94, 114, 122, 152
  Properties 150
Foo Kee General Store 40, 59, 82, 114. See also Chinese General Store
Foo Kee property 62
Foothill Resources, Ltd. 183
Foreign Miners' Tax 19, 37, 40, 68
Fortune Peaceful Gambling House 118, 126, 129
Fou Sin 23, 24, 25, 26, 27, 28
Funerals 109
Fung Fong 118, 126, 131, 133

G

Ga Gum Yuk 89
Gamblers
  Fiddletown 96, 118
  Ione 101
  Jackson 100
Gambling 98, 117, 129
Garavaglia, Michael 187
Garavalia Architecture, Inc. 187
Gardens. See Chinese gardens
Geary Act 128, 139
Gist, William Thornton 40

Gist, W.T. 51, 61
Goff, David Martin 39
Goff, Mary 40, 51
Gold 8, 16, 55, 64
Gold mines 64
Gold Mountain 11, 41, 57, 62, 77, 98, 124, 130, 131
Gold Rush 8, 16, 188
Governor's Historic Preservation Award 185, 187
Graveyards. See Cemeteries; See Cemeteries
Griswold, Martin Van Buren 22, 26
Guangdong Province 25, 36, 48, 53, 77, 84, 131, 176
Guangzhou 11, 54, 91, 133

H

Head, James 61
Hellman, Anne 186
Herbal medicine 42, 44, 49, 50, 118, 130
Heungshan 12, 78, 113, 155
Historic preservation 179
Hog pen ordinance 73
Hoiping 155
Hong Kong 11, 54, 97, 131, 158
Hop Wah Chung 53, 56, 142, 145
Huiguans. See District associations
Hungry Ghosts Festival 109

I

Ideal Basic Industries 180
Immigration Act of 1965 147
Imports. See Trade
Ione 9, 26, 66, 71, 72, 74, 82, 145
  Chinese population 34, 63, 71, 95
  Property ownership 53

J

Jackson 9, 22, 26, 32, 68, 72, 74, 84, 87, 90, 103, 114, 144, 153, 173
  Chinese population 63, 71, 95
  Flood 70
  Property ownership 52
Jackson Creek 32, 53, 70
Jackson Gate 32
Jeng Ting 158
Joss house. See Temple

Jow Moke 163. See also Yee (Mrs. Jow Moke)
Jow Moke, Mrs.. See Yee (Mrs. Jow Moke)

K

Kai Kee 142, 145
Kilham, Horace 23, 26, 28
Kum Yow 150
Kutchenthal, Henry Augustus 48, 79
Kwong, Ken 30
Ky Kee 53, 56

L

Labor unions 64, 67
Lancha Plana 9, 32, 72
  Chinese population 34, 95
  Property ownership 53
Lang 38, 39
Laundries 73, 75, 148
Lawrence, Bob 136, 168
Lawrence, Mary 168, 171
Lee, Art 174
Lee Kee 51, 57, 114, 122, 148
Limestone quarry controversy 180
Lion dance 88
Lottery tickets. See Pigeon tickets
Lott, Tommy 163

M

Man Lung & Co. 123
Mare Island 163
Marriage 14
  China 132
Marriages 91
Martell, Louis 16
Marvin, Judith 183, 184, 186
Marysville 23, 54
McDanel, Carl 187
McGlashan, Charles 73
Merchand, Charles 30
Merchandise stores 54, 59, 118
Merchants 71, 110
  Drytown 52, 56
  Fiddletown 37, 51, 57, 58, 77, 114

Ione 53, 56, 142
    Jackson 53, 56
    Partnership documents 141
    Plymouth 56
    Volcano 56
Mid-Autumn Festival 104
Miners 16, 37, 77, 80, 94
Miners' League 64
Ming 147
Mokelumne Hill 144
Mokelumne River 8, 16, 53, 66
Mooncakes 105
Morena Vineyard 165
Morgan, James 65
Mui [Mooey] family 142

N

Namhoi 113
National Hotel 173
National Park Service 181
New Chicago 108
Newton Copper Mine 66
Ngan Chew. See Chew Kee
Ngan Chow Sing 124

O

Oakland Museum 184
Oleta. See Fiddletown
Oleta School 129
Oneida Mine 65
On Hop 52, 56
On Yee 77
Opium 59, 91, 97, 119, 146, 183
Order of Caucasians 68, 98

P

Page Act 91, 156
Pai gow 98
Pearl River Delta 11, 16, 78, 84
Pharmacy. See Herbal medicine
Pigeon, Joseph 136
Pigeon tickets 99, 118
Placer mining 8, 18, 41, 64, 80

Plymouth 10, 32, 68, 70, 74, 80, 103, 139, 147, 168
Poll tax 20, 68
Prostitutes 37, 90, 94, 95, 113, 117, 129, 156
Punyu 53, 85, 89, 113, 117, 120, 127, 149, 157
Punyu Association 153
Purinton, Columbus A. 17

Q

Qing Dynasty 11, 15, 87, 120, 124, 129, 132, 136
Qingming 109
Qu Yuan 103

R

Railroad, transcontinental. See Central Pacific Railroad
Rammed earth 41, 46
Rammed Earth 180
Rammed Earth Works 184
Raphael, Meyer 39
Ratto's Law Collection Agency 123
Ray, Elizabeth 39
Ray, William 39
Resistance by Chinese 68, 72, 80, 140
Richards, Spencer 36
Rosenwald & Kahn 168
Russell, Jane 184

S

Sacramento 15, 48, 49, 50, 54, 63, 89, 110, 124, 139, 160, 164, 170, 176
Sacramento Pioneer Association 177
Sammy's Café 174
Sam Yup 12, 78, 117, 127, 155
Sam Yup Association 84, 165
San Francisco 15, 18, 26, 54, 56, 63, 67, 89, 97, 107, 110, 124, 131, 133, 139, 158, 164, 169, 180
  Chinese population 37
San Joaquin Delta College 184
Schallhorn, Christopher 46
Schoonover, Albert 179
Scofield, Marie 181
Scott Act 71, 93, 141
Shenandoah Valley 37
Shunduk 113
Sigh Choy 79, 96, 113, 117, 120, 125, 126, 157, 166, 184

Simpson, E.C. 52, 122
Sing Choy 59, 94, 113
Sing Kee 56
Sing Tong village 41, 177
Sing Wo. See Wo Sing
Spinetti brothers 145
Stanford, Jane 49
Stanford, Leland 49
Stanley, Dick 186
Stockton 15, 26, 54, 132, 146, 163, 164, 165, 168, 176
Sunning. See Toishan
Sunwui 157
Sun Yatsen 87, 125
Sutter Canal & Mining Company 66
Sutter Creek 9, 32, 65, 67, 72, 98
Symbolism 46, 106
Sze Yup 12, 78, 155
Sze Yup Association 84, 101

T

Tai'ping Rebellion 12
Temple
  Drytown 108
  Fiddletown 149
  Jackson 106, 144
Toishan 12, 41, 63, 78, 113, 157, 173, 177
Tongs 86, 90
Trade 97
  China 43, 54, 71, 118, 140
Treaty of Nanjing 11
Truckee 73
Tse Duk 155
Tung Paeng 56
Tuolumne County 19, 24, 54

U

Uhlinger, Frank 122
Union Hotel 36, 39, 41, 52
University of the Pacific
  School of Dentristy 176
  School of Pharmacy 184
U.S. Institute of Museum and Library Services 184

V

Virginia City 48
Volcano 9, 32, 51, 146
  Chinese population 71

W

Wah Hing. See Yee Lok Sam
Water ditches 17, 66
Weaverville 85, 108
Wey, Nancy 182
Women 90, 94, 113, 135, 144
  China 13, 93
  Fiddletown 53
Wong, Anna May 171
Wong Bok Yue 133
Won, Joseph 145
Woolfolk, Elsie 165
Workingmens' Party 67
Wo Sing 39, 51, 57, 61, 77, 114, 125, 148

X

Xianggang. See Hong Kong

Y

Yates, E.R. 39
Yee Chow Sung 157
Yee Duk 49
Yee Family Association 185
Yee Fung 51, 117, 122, 125, 149
  business 49
  properties 48
Yee Fung Cheung 41, 45, 51, 184
Yee, Henry 176
Yee, Herbert K. 49, 170, 176, 181, 182, 187
Yee, Johnny 170
Yee King Cheung 49
Yee Kuan Wo 157
Yee Lee Sai Ngun 49
Yee Lok Sam 48, 49, 50, 176
Yee (Mrs. Jow Moke) 130, 131, 148, 163, 165
Yee Sing Wo 157
Yee Way Duk. See Yee, Henry

Yee, Wesley 176
Yee Wun 157
Yee Yuke 157
Yee Yun 49
Ye [Ge] Lung 67
Yep, May 174
Yep, Som 173
Yeung Sing 131, 132
Young China 133

Z

Zhongshan. See Heungshan
Zhu Liao village 127, 131